THE TREASURE BOOK OF CLUJ

projectograph
cluj • 2016

Table of Contents

Introduction ... 3

II-IIIrd Century. *The Roman Napoca* ... 4

IV – IXth Century. *Migrants Among The Ruins* ... 6

Xth Century. *Village Of The Conquering Hungarians* ... 8

XI – XIIIth Century. *The Birth Of The City* ... 10

XIVth Century. *The City Comes To Life* ... 12

XVth Century. *The Free Royal City* ... 16

XVIth Century. *The Treasure City* ... 20

XVIIth Century. *Heyday and Decline* ... 24

XVIIIth Century. *Under Habsburg Rule* ... 28

The First Half of the XIXth Century. *Reforms and Revolution* ... 32

The Second Half of the XIXth Century. *Peace and Prosperity* ... 36

The Beginning of the XXth Century. *Life at the Turn of the Century* ... 40

From the 1920s to 1940s. *Between Two World Wars* ... 44

The Second Half of the XXth Century. *The Concrete City* ... 48

The Beginning of the XXIst Century and the Future. *A European City* ... 52

Glossary ... 56

Dear Reader,

If you start to read this book, you'll set off on an extraordinary time travel adventure. We'll take you to the Roman Napoca of two thousand years ago, then to the village of the conquering Hungarians, and later to the fortress of Cluj besieged by the Mongols, yet all the while we won't leave the city that today we call Cluj. In these fourteen chapters you will learn of the birth of the city in the Middle Ages, following its development from one century to the next, right up to the present. The final chapter tells us of the Cluj of today and of the future.

We have tried to write and draw everything as precisely as possible. This has not always been easy, because even a historian – just like a good detective – relies on small pieces of evidence when he tries to reconstruct buildings or events of the past. If this book had been written twenty years ago, the chapters about the Roman period, about migration, and about the conquering Hungarians would have looked different, because archeologists have made new discoveries since then. So it might well happen that newer archaeological excavations will uncover things that will later change our image of Cluj's history.

We want you to come to know and love the city better, the city where perhaps you were born, or live, or where you have come as a visitor. Maybe this is your first time here, or maybe you have been here often. We have selected a few out of the city's many treasures for you: famous people, important buildings, old streets and squares, exciting stories and inventions. Altogether these form what we proudly call the Treasure City or, more modestly, Cluj. There should be just enough here to put you in the mood for exploring by yourself. Not even a book ten times thicker could hold all the treasures of the city. However, we hope that after you have finished reading the book, you will want to start searching for further treasures.

While reading, you might find an encyclopedia helpful. The more difficult words are in *italics*, and you can find their meaning in the glossary at the end of the book.

In the name of all the creators of the book, I wish you a time travel rich in treasures.

The Editor

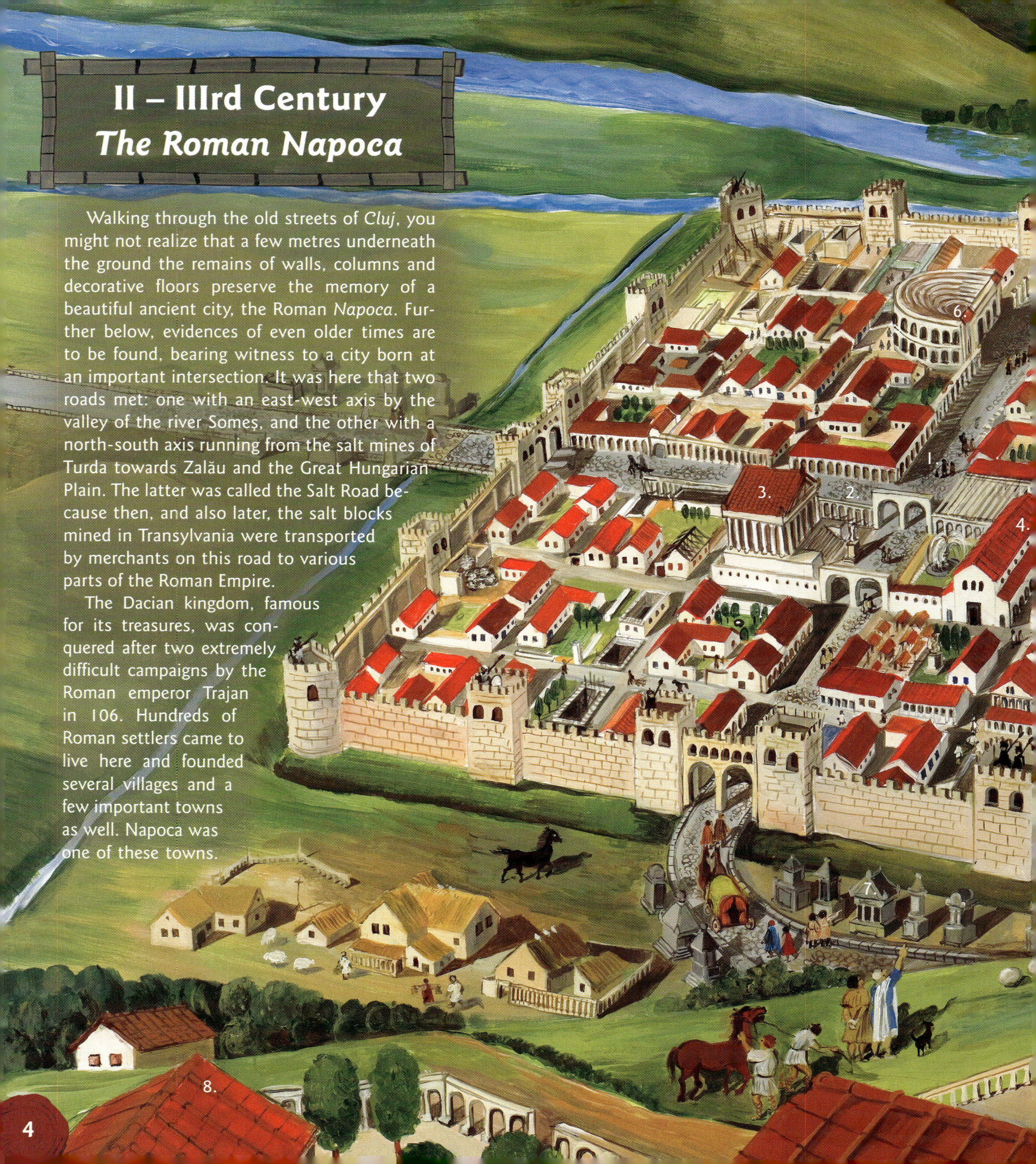

II – IIIrd Century
The Roman Napoca

Walking through the old streets of *Cluj*, you might not realize that a few metres underneath the ground the remains of walls, columns and decorative floors preserve the memory of a beautiful ancient city, the Roman *Napoca*. Further below, evidences of even older times are to be found, bearing witness to a city born at an important intersection. It was here that two roads met: one with an east-west axis by the valley of the river Someș, and the other with a north-south axis running from the salt mines of Turda towards Zalău and the Great Hungarian Plain. The latter was called the Salt Road because then, and also later, the salt blocks mined in Transylvania were transported by merchants on this road to various parts of the Roman Empire.

The Dacian kingdom, famous for its treasures, was conquered after two extremely difficult campaigns by the Roman emperor Trajan in 106. Hundreds of Roman settlers came to live here and founded several villages and a few important towns as well. Napoca was one of these towns.

Originally it was a modest settlement located near the bridge that crossed the Someș at the foot of the Citadel that still stands there today. The settlement was so favourably situated that in less than fifteen years a flourishing Roman town was built here. The streets of the new town were as straight as if they had been drawn with a ruler. The Romans called the two main roads which intersected each other by the same names in every town or city: Cardo Maximus and Decumanus Maximus. The Forum, or the center of the town, was at the intersection of the two merchant roads, approximately at the site of the present-day St. Michael's Church, and there the *capitolium*, a temple, was built in honour of the three major Roman gods: Jupiter, Juno and Minerva. The *basilica*, the predecessor of the law court, was built at the Forum too, opposite the temple. In the building called the *praetorium*, the *proconsul* of the emperor had his residence. The town also had the usual popular meeting and entertainment places of the Romans: the baths, the theatre and the *amphitheatre*.

Napoca was considered a medium-sized, but rich Roman town whose inhabitants consisted not only of soldiers, but also of artisans and wealthy merchants. The rich citizens had slaves and owned lands and rural houses – *villa rustica* – outside the town.

Beginning with the second half of the 3rd century, due to changes in climate and increasing attacks from outside the Empire, the Romans completely evacuated the town.

1. Cardo Maximus; 2. Decumanus Maximus; 3. capitolium; 4. basilica; 5. praetorium; 6. theatre; 7. cemetery; 8. villa rustica.

IV – IXth Century
Migrants Among The Ruins

In 271 Emperor Aurelian resettled not only the Roman army, but also Napoca's civilian inhabitants, to a province on the southern side of the Danube. In the abandoned territories, only a small number of *Dacians* remained, living in the mountains.

The Visigoths
Soon most of Transylvania was occupied by the *Visigoths*. For a short century, they lived near the ruined Napoca until the *Huns* arrived from Central Asia and ended their rule.

1. Gepid market

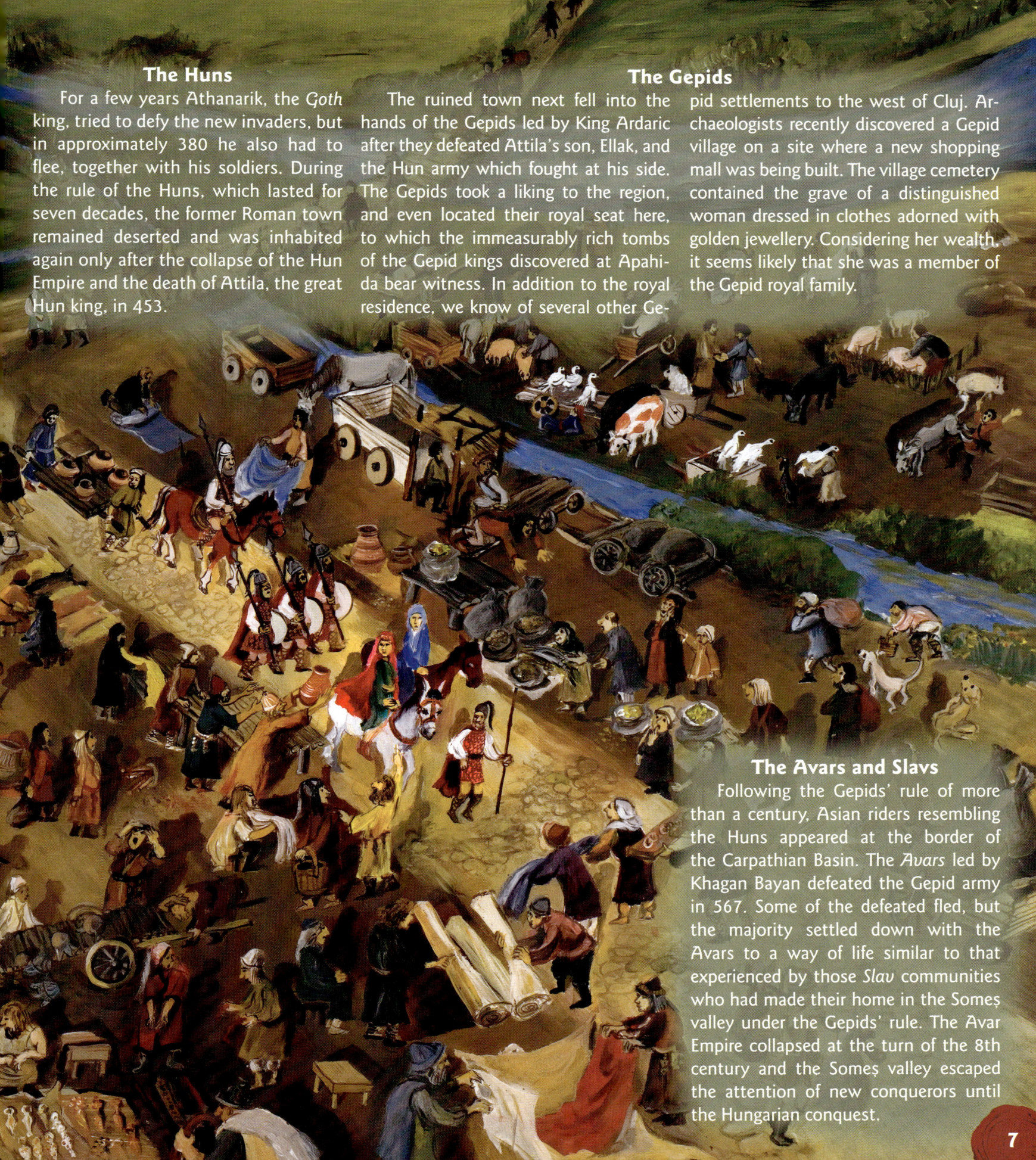

The Huns

For a few years Athanarik, the *Goth* king, tried to defy the new invaders, but in approximately 380 he also had to flee, together with his soldiers. During the rule of the Huns, which lasted for seven decades, the former Roman town remained deserted and was inhabited again only after the collapse of the Hun Empire and the death of Attila, the great Hun king, in 453.

The Gepids

The ruined town next fell into the hands of the Gepids led by King Ardaric after they defeated Attila's son, Ellak, and the Hun army which fought at his side. The Gepids took a liking to the region, and even located their royal seat here, to which the immeasurably rich tombs of the Gepid kings discovered at Apahida bear witness. In addition to the royal residence, we know of several other Gepid settlements to the west of Cluj. Archaeologists recently discovered a Gepid village on a site where a new shopping mall was being built. The village cemetery contained the grave of a distinguished woman dressed in clothes adorned with golden jewellery. Considering her wealth, it seems likely that she was a member of the Gepid royal family.

The Avars and Slavs

Following the Gepids' rule of more than a century, Asian riders resembling the Huns appeared at the border of the Carpathian Basin. The *Avars* led by Khagan Bayan defeated the Gepid army in 567. Some of the defeated fled, but the majority settled down with the Avars to a way of life similar to that experienced by those *Slav* communities who had made their home in the Someș valley under the Gepids' rule. The Avar Empire collapsed at the turn of the 8th century and the Someș valley escaped the attention of new conquerors until the Hungarian conquest.

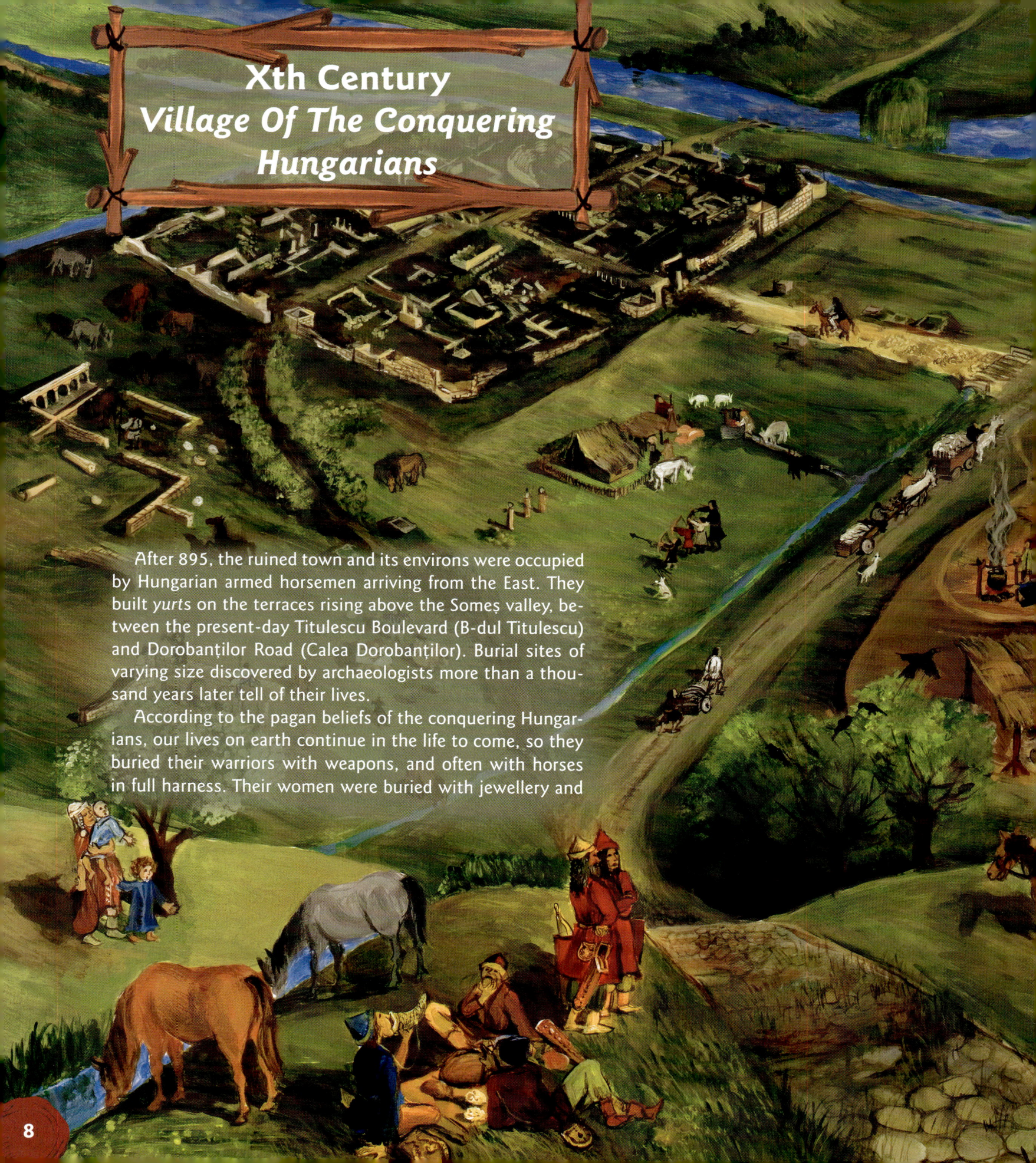

Xth Century
Village Of The Conquering Hungarians

After 895, the ruined town and its environs were occupied by Hungarian armed horsemen arriving from the East. They built *yurt*s on the terraces rising above the Someș valley, between the present-day Titulescu Boulevard (B-dul Titulescu) and Dorobanților Road (Calea Dorobanților). Burial sites of varying size discovered by archaeologists more than a thousand years later tell of their lives.

According to the pagan beliefs of the conquering Hungarians, our lives on earth continue in the life to come, so they buried their warriors with weapons, and often with horses in full harness. Their women were buried with jewellery and small utensils, and their children with *amulet*s to protect them from evil spirits. In the graves of poor people, by contrast, only a knife or a *spindle whorl* or perhaps nothing at all was found. Judging by the excavated graves in Cluj, the Hungarians who settled here were mainly soldiers who fought using sabres and bows. Their main task was to guard and defend the intersection of the two main roads mentioned in the first chapter.

In the vicinity of the active duty soldiers, ordinary people lived their everyday lives peacefully. Children gathering around the workshops of blacksmiths, potters, goldsmiths, *coopers*, and saddle and bow makers, watched the craftsmen's' quick movements. In addition to hunting, off-duty soldiers taught the local children just as the craftsmen did. During their common games boys, almost unconsciously, learnt how to ride a horse, or use a bow or a sabre. Girls learnt from older women not only how to cook and bake, but also how to build a yurt. The provisioning of the village was managed by ordinary people, including fishers, hunters and farmers.

1. dug-out (a house dug partially into the ground);
2. yurt; 3. cemetery.

XI – XIIIth Century
The Birth Of The City

The fortress and monastery of Cluj

The story of Cluj in the Middle Ages began not in the centre of the present city, but at the *monastery* west of it. Soon after the year 1000, King Saint Stephen built a strong fortress here, traces of which are still visible, out of mud and wood. This fortress was seen as the centre of Cluj county and it was here that the *bailiff* representing the interests of the king resided. A hundred years later King Saint Ladislaus founded a monastery for the *Benedictine order* inside this protected location. Thanks to royal donations, the *monks* became so rich that their power equalled that of the Transylvanian bishop. As a result, in approximately the year 1200, Bishop Adorján and his men attacked the monks and imprisoned them, and the monastery was severely damaged. The surviving monks suffered an even more terrible blow in 1241. The army of the dreaded *Mongols* approached the fortress in which the population of nearby settlements had also taken refuge. Resistance in the face of the enemy's numerical superiority was in vain. The Mongols occupied the fortress, killed the inhabitants, and demolished the monastery. Everything was left in ruins for many decades, and it was only in approximately 1300 that the monks were able to build a new church. The *sanctuary* of the church has been preserved and stands in the present-day neighbourhood of Mănăştur on Calvary Hill.

The formation of the city

In the 11th and 12th centuries, not far from the fortress of Cluj and somewhere near the present-day city centre, there was a small village. Since maps were not made at the time, we don't know its exact location. However, during archaeological excavations the village's cemetery was found underneath the current main square of the city, *Piața* Unirii. As was the custom, the dead were buried in their most beautiful clothes and adorned with jewellery, so these recently uncovered graves tell us a lot about these former inhabitants of Cluj.

In 1241 the Mongol hordes destroyed not only the fortress, but also the village, leaving ruined houses and burnt fields behind them. In order to encourage repopulation of the area, King Stephen V awarded certain *privilege*s to those who settled there. Most of the new settlers were Saxons. Thanks to their diligence and enterprising spirit, on the site of what later came to be called the Old Town, the medieval city of Cluj was built.

1. fortress;
2. Benedictine Monastery and Church;
3. Cluj.

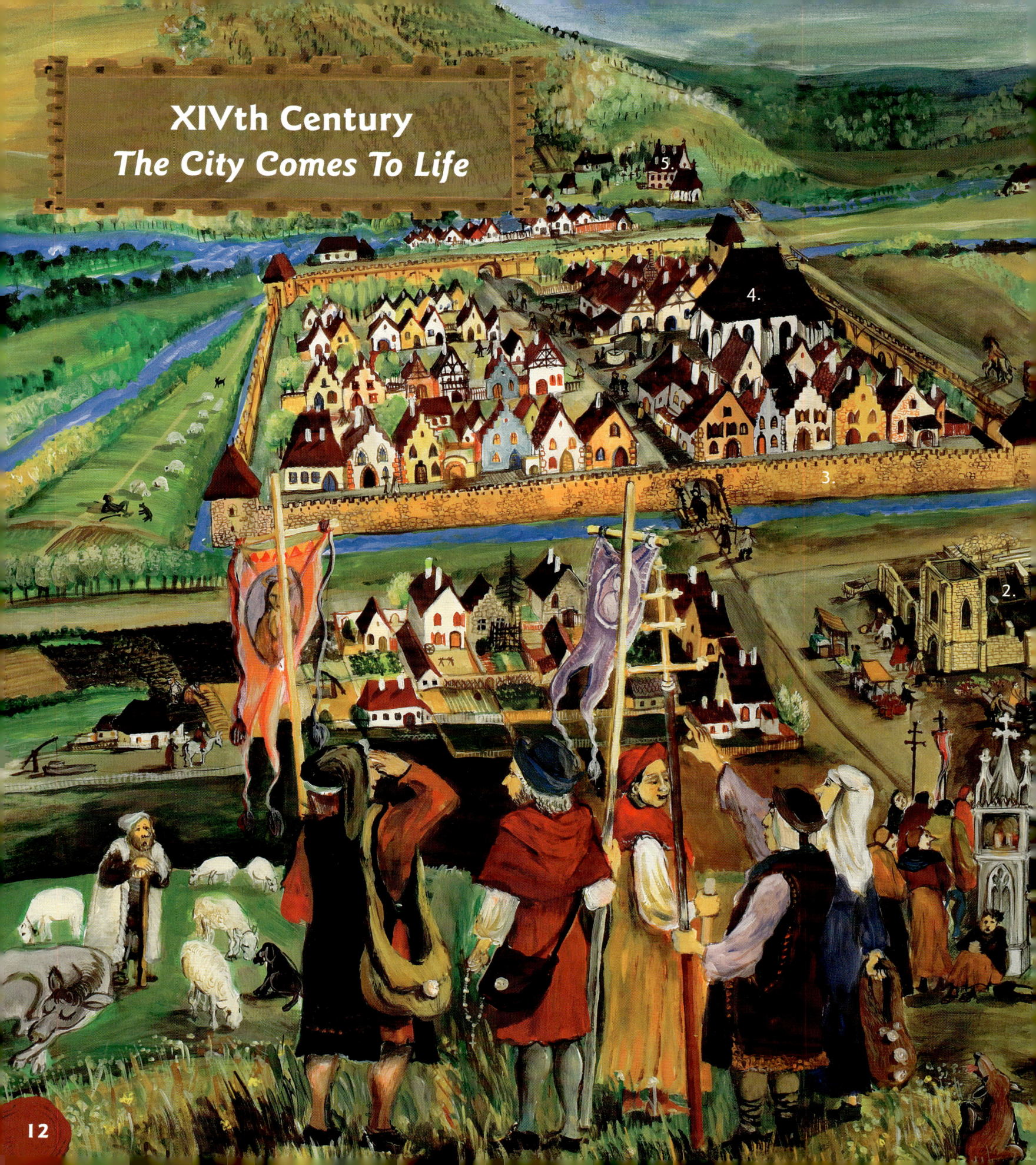

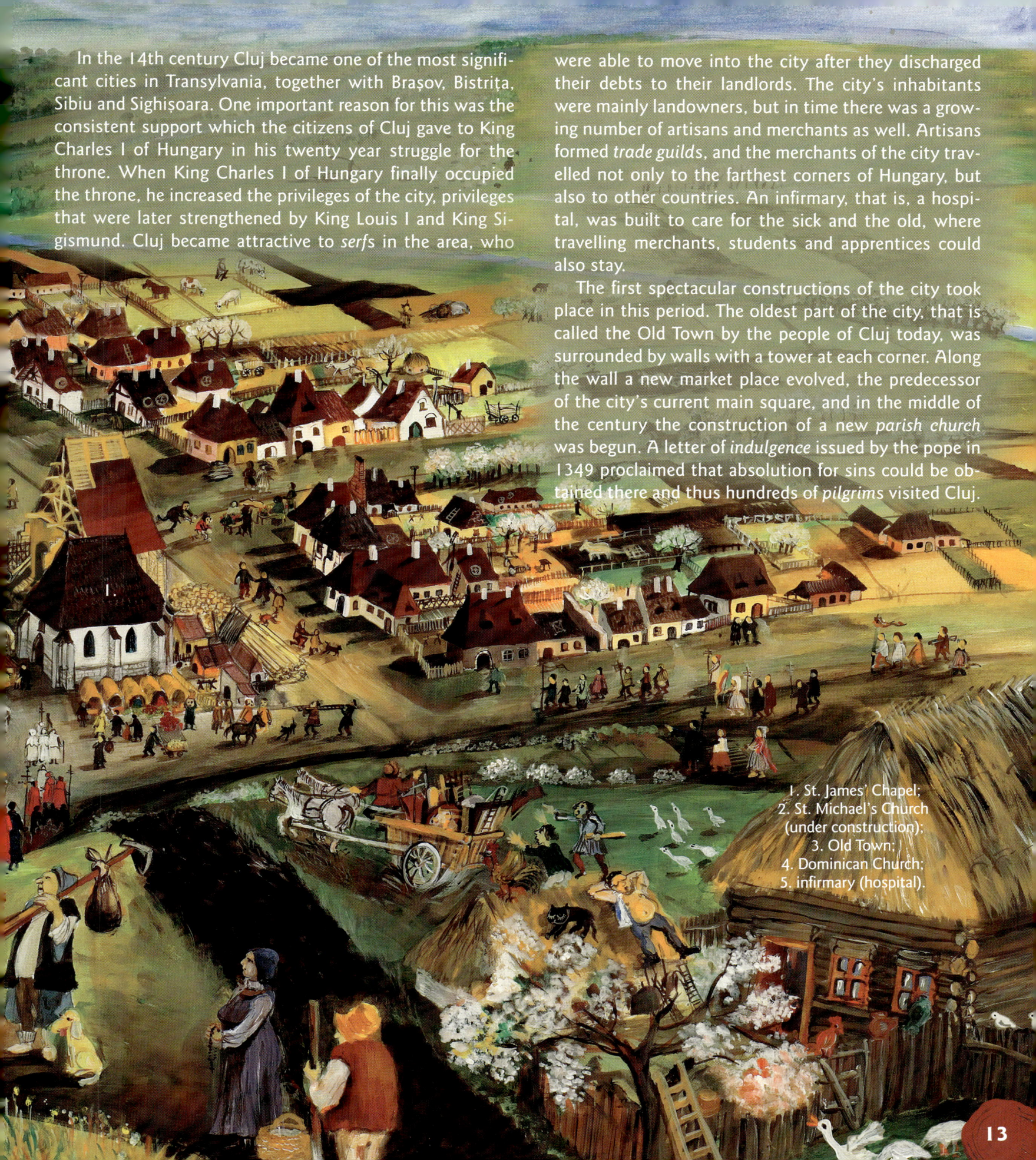

In the 14th century Cluj became one of the most significant cities in Transylvania, together with Brașov, Bistrița, Sibiu and Sighișoara. One important reason for this was the consistent support which the citizens of Cluj gave to King Charles I of Hungary in his twenty year struggle for the throne. When King Charles I of Hungary finally occupied the throne, he increased the privileges of the city, privileges that were later strengthened by King Louis I and King Sigismund. Cluj became attractive to *serf*s in the area, who were able to move into the city after they discharged their debts to their landlords. The city's inhabitants were mainly landowners, but in time there was a growing number of artisans and merchants as well. Artisans formed *trade guild*s, and the merchants of the city travelled not only to the farthest corners of Hungary, but also to other countries. An infirmary, that is, a hospital, was built to care for the sick and the old, where travelling merchants, students and apprentices could also stay.

The first spectacular constructions of the city took place in this period. The oldest part of the city, that is called the Old Town by the people of Cluj today, was surrounded by walls with a tower at each corner. Along the wall a new market place evolved, the predecessor of the city's current main square, and in the middle of the century the construction of a new *parish church* was begun. A letter of *indulgence* issued by the pope in 1349 proclaimed that absolution for sins could be obtained there and thus hundreds of *pilgrim*s visited Cluj.

1. St. James' Chapel;
2. St. Michael's Church (under construction);
3. Old Town;
4. Dominican Church;
5. infirmary (hospital).

1316. The citizens of Cluj receive new city privileges

At the end of August 1316, Cluj celebrated when Benedek, the parish priest, came directly from the king, bringing with him a decoratively sealed *charter*. Showing his gratitude for the faithfulness of its citizens, King Charles I had granted city privileges to Cluj. This was an important moment in the history of the city and it was fittingly celebrated by rich and poor alike. The proclamation of the contents of the charter (below) was the big draw of the celebration:

1. Citizens may elect freely a judge who can resolve matters under dispute.
2. Likewise, the parish priest of the city may be elected freely.
3. The merchants of the city are free from taxes within the borders of Transylvania.
4. Citizens owning a house and land must pay 52 silver marks annually.
5. Groups of sixty families are obliged to equip a soldier and send him to the king's army.

1367. Feleacu, the guard village

The main road connecting Turda with Cluj was one of the busiest commercial roads in Transylvania. Ruffians and bandits hiding in Feleacu Forest often attacked merchants who were travelling with valuable cargos. In 1367 Louis the Great permitted the citizens of Cluj to resettle twenty Romanian families, whose task it was to guard this part of the road, at the top of Feleacu Hill. This is the first reference to the presence and role of Romanians in the life of Cluj.

1373. Cluj Brothers

In 1373 two Cluj brothers, György and Márton, made a golden *bronze* equestrian statue that was unsurpassed in its beauty throughout all of Europe. The original statue can be seen in Prague, but a copy now stands in front of the Central *Reformed Church* on Kogălniceanu (formerly, Farkas) Street. The statue represents Saint George, the embodiment of Christian knightly virtues, plunging his spear into the neck of a dragon. The two eminent master craftsmen grew up and were educated in Cluj, where their artistic personality developed in the workshop of their father, Miklós, who was a talented painter and whose workshop was responsible for painting *altars*, *devotional pictures*, and statues for the churches of the city and the surrounding area. Márton and György learnt the first tricks of their trade in this workshop and ended up outshining their father's talent and fame by far.

1377. The first seal of the city

The freedom and prestige of a medieval city was evidenced not only by its charter, but also by its seal. The latter meant that the city could issue official documents that were recognized throughout the entire kingdom. Cluj received the right to use such a seal from Louis the Great in 1377. The seal's *wax impression* has been preserved on certain documents to this day and depicts a fortress wall with three towers and a gate with a partly raised *portcullis*.

XVth Century
The Free Royal City

1. house of the parish priest; 2. birthplace of King Matthias; 3. Dominican Monastery; 4. gate tower on Regele Ferdinand Street; 5. small gate (the current Fire Tower) on Tipografiei Street; 6. gate tower on December 21, 1989 Boulevard (B-dul 21 Decembrie 1989); 7. Potters' Tower;

The appearance of Cluj had changed immensely by the end of the 15th century. Privileges gained in previous centuries had advanced the life of the city. In 1405 King Sigismund, later the Holy Roman Emperor, raised Cluj to the rank of a free royal city, and permitted the enclosure of the new town district next to the Old Town. Life within the walls under construction was noisy. Rich merchants arrived and departed through the new gates. Workshops of tailors, goldsmiths, and potters were opened one after the other. Trade guilds were responsible for maintaining and guarding the fortress walls and towers. Constructions became a permanent sight on the city's squares and streets. Saint Michael's Church was being built, as well as the *Dominican* and *Franciscan* Monasteries and a string of new houses. The city had a population of almost 4,000 people, half of them Saxon, half Hungarian. The new fortress wall was completed by the end of the century, and its eighteen towers proclaimed from afar to approaching travellers that this was a rich and powerful city.

8. gate tower on Eroilor Street; 9. Tailors' Tower; 10. sentry-box; 11. Central Reformed Church; 12. Masons' Tower; 13. gate tower on Turzii Road (Calea Turzii); 14. Carpenters' Tower; 15. Shoemakers' Tower; 16. gate tower on Mănăştur Road (Calea Mănăştur); 17. Blacksmiths' Tower; 18. Goldsmiths' Tower; 19. mill.

1437. Peasant revolt in the Cluj district

In 1437 a strong peasant uprising shook what had been a relatively peaceful period in Transylvania. Peasants armed with scythes and pitchforks gathered on Mount Bobâlna north of Cluj and demanded reduced taxes and freedom of movement. They built a camp at Bobâlna and under the leadership of Antal Nagy de Buda they successfully defeated the noblemen's troops sent against them. During the winter, the rebels found refuge behind the walls of Cluj. Emerging from the city, they fought with the noblemen's army at the village of Cluj-Mănăștur (the present-day Mănăștur neighbourhood). Antal Nagy de Buda died in the battle and the uprising was suppressed. As a punishment for offering shelter to the rebels, Cluj was deprived of some of its privileges. These were restored only seven years later by King Vladislaus I.

1443. The birth of Matthias

On a cold day at the end of February, vine-grower Jakab Méhfi was given the greatest honour of his life. In one of the comfortable rooms of his house in the Old Town, Matthias, the second son of Erzsébet Szilágyi and János Hunyadi, was born. The fate of the house has been determined by this event over the centuries. In 1467 King Matthias absolved the house of his birth and all properties belonging to it from any tax liabilities. As a sign of gratitude toward their just ruler, the owners of the house decorated its doors and windows with the Hunyadi coat of arms depicting a raven.

1455. Life in the Dominican Monastery

In the second half of the 15th century a huge *Gothic* church and monastery was built in the north-eastern corner of the Old Town for the Dominican monks. *Friar*s dressed in white gowns and black, hooded cloaks meditated and prayed the *Liturgy of the Hours* within its walls or walked the city streets. They busied themselves with teaching or *evangelizing* the local citizens, and in exchange they received *alms*. Three times a day they ate a modest meal together in the spacious *refectory* of the monastery. As they ate, one of them would read aloud the Bible from an ornate niche built in the wall of the dining area. The friars made vows of permanent poverty, so they had no private income. Their rich monastery was built thanks to the donations of rich city people. János Hunyadi, the fighter of the Turks and Matthias's father, was Hungary's governor and one of their donors. Every year, beginning in 1455, he gave a large amount of salt to the friars, who sold it and used the money to build the monastery.

Matthias and the Cluj judge

According to legend, on hearing that the poor were being oppressed in his country, and especially in his birthplace of Cluj, Matthias set off in disguise. Arriving to Cluj, he walked straight to the main square, to the judge's house. From here he could see many poor people carrying wood to the judge's yard, where they then cut it. Soldiers, using sticks, prodded them on in their work. Suddenly one of the soldiers caught sight of King Matthias and shouted at him, "Hey, you there! Why are you wasting the day? You've a face as long as a fiddle. Get up, you nasty fellow!" He even gave him a blow with his stick. Matthias got up, but he did not begin working. Instead, he asked how much he would be paid. Another blow was the answer. He started carrying some wood and, when no one was looking, he marked three logs with red chalk. In the evening he walked away quietly, but the next day he returned to the city, this time dressed in royal robes. When he got to the judge's yard, he asked him who had brought the

enormous amount of wood there. The judge smiled and said that the poor helped him out of love. Matthias told the soldiers to scatter the logs, and when he found the ones he had marked, he ordered the cruel judge to be whipped.

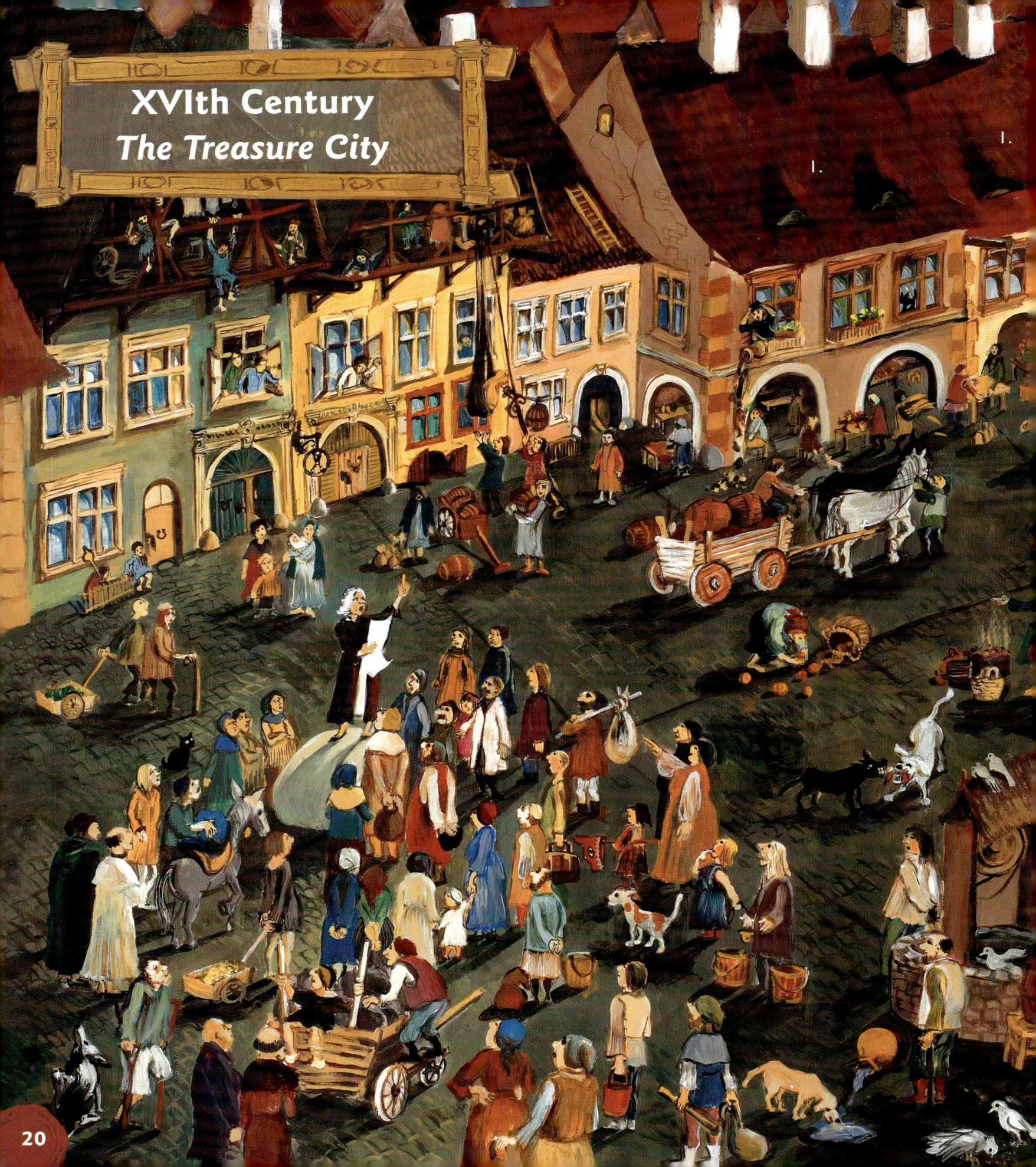

In the second half of the 16th century, after the establishment of the Transylvanian *Principality*, Cluj began to develop rapidly. *Renaissance* houses, one more beautiful than the next, were built on the northern side of the main square and the bustling life of the city unfolded before them. Shoppers and merchants bargained, sampled wines, and selected expensive fabrics. By this time Cluj, with its 9,500 inhabitants, was Transylvania's most populated city. Thanks to its clever merchants and talented artisans, it had become the most important and richest city, a real "treasure city" of the Principality.

In the middle of the century the *Reformation* reached Cluj, and part of the population left the *Roman Catholic Church* and became first *Lutheran* and later *Reformed*. Still others became *Unitarian*. In fact, the Unitarian Church was founded right here in Cluj. *Pastor* Ferenc Dávid, standing on a big, round rock in the main square, gave such a powerful speech to the people gathered round him, that many of both the Saxons and the Hungarians became Unitarians.

1. arcaded houses.

St. Michael's Church

The building of St. Michael's Church in the main square of the city had begun in the 14th century, but it was finished only at the beginning of the 16th century. The spacious interior of the church was decorated with an elegant stone *pulpit* and painted, carved altars and statues. Coloured images on the walls depicted Biblical scenes and the most important saints. However, according to the teachings of the Reformation, churches had to be cleansed of images and statues and St. Michael's did not escape. Its wall images were covered over with white paint and its altars and statues were removed. Yet the significance of St. Michael's Church did not decrease throughout the centuries. Three monarchs of the Principality, who bore the title of prince, were elected within its walls, and the *Transylvanian Diet* was held there thirty-six times.

Beginning in the 16th century, Gipsy families settled on the outskirts of the city came to be responsible for the cleaning of the streets.

1550. Gáspár Heltai's printing press

Gáspár Heltai, a Saxon born, educated *Protestant* preacher and a pastor of the Saxon Church in Cluj, founded his own printing press in his house. Setting up the printing press took a very long time. First he brought beautiful, new lead types from Germany and trained apprentices. Then he bought paper and a big quantity of lead. Since paper was very rare and expensive at that time, he later built his own *paper-mill* and produced materials for printing there. Many beautifully decorated books were printed by his press, including the first Hungarian school books, hymn books, fables and history books. Gáspár Heltai is credited as being the first to regularize spelling when printing books.

1581. The first college in Transylvania

For years István Báthory, Transylvania's Catholic prince, had been planning to establish a college in Transylvania. On becoming acquainted with the teaching methods of *Jesuit* monks in Poland, he decided to bring them to Transylvania to found a college in Cluj. However, this turned out not to be an easy task in a city where the majority of the people had turned to Unitarianism.

In 1581 the prince gave the Jesuits the empty Franciscan Monastery and founded the Jesuit College. He also supported financially the building of a *boarding school*. The Jesuit monastic order sent excellent teachers to Cluj, not only from Hungarian territories, but also from the far corners of Europe, so that Transylvania's first college had Polish, German, Italian and French teachers as well.

However, Transylvanian students were not to enjoy the education of the Jesuits for long. The order was expelled from Transylvania, and although they returned a few years later, in 1603 they were chased out again by the citizens of the city. This time their buildings were damaged, and so the activities of the first college in Cluj came to a halt.

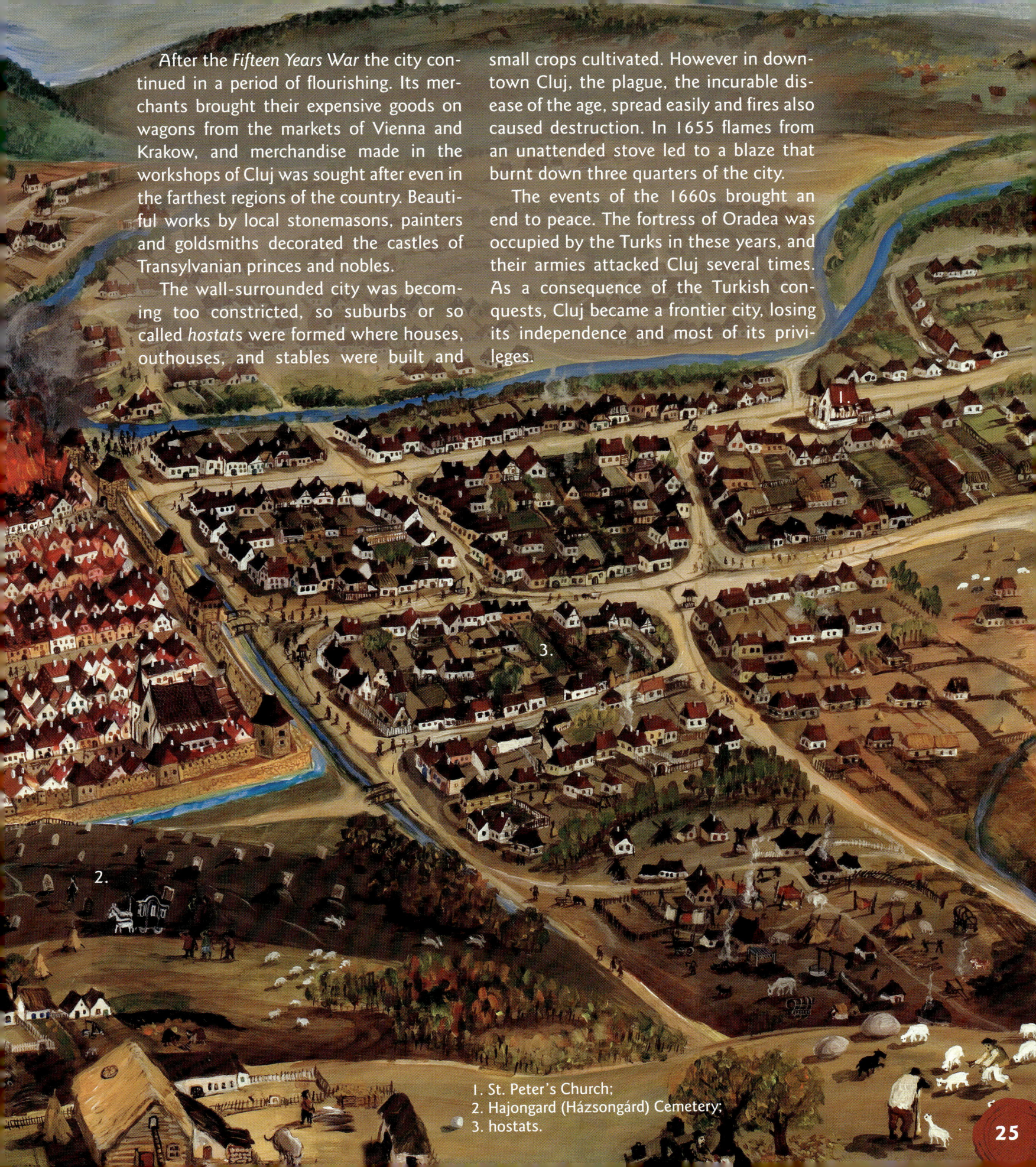

After the *Fifteen Years War* the city continued in a period of flourishing. Its merchants brought their expensive goods on wagons from the markets of Vienna and Krakow, and merchandise made in the workshops of Cluj was sought after even in the farthest regions of the country. Beautiful works by local stonemasons, painters and goldsmiths decorated the castles of Transylvanian princes and nobles.

The wall-surrounded city was becoming too constricted, so suburbs or so called *hostat*s were formed where houses, outhouses, and stables were built and small crops cultivated. However in downtown Cluj, the plague, the incurable disease of the age, spread easily and fires also caused destruction. In 1655 flames from an unattended stove led to a blaze that burnt down three quarters of the city.

The events of the 1660s brought an end to peace. The fortress of Oradea was occupied by the Turks in these years, and their armies attacked Cluj several times. As a consequence of the Turkish conquests, Cluj became a frontier city, losing its independence and most of its privileges.

1. St. Peter's Church;
2. Hajongard (Házsongárd) Cemetery;
3. hostats.

The city council

Decisions about important issues regarding the life of the city were made by the *judge royal* and a *chief judge* who were elected yearly by the so called council of one hundred. If in any given year the judge royal was a Hungarian, the chief judge, by law, had to be Saxon.

Their meetings were held in the council-hall on the south-eastern corner of the main square. Its walls were decorated with inscriptions and figures related to justice and moderation, reminding the council members of the importance of just governance.

After Cluj became a frontier city the prince named a military commander to govern it, instead of elected leaders, with *garrison* troops to serve under him.

Beginning in 1585, the bodies of several thousand killed by the plague which devastated the city were taken to the new cemetery, Hajongard.

1647. Inauguration of the Central Reformed Church

From the beginning of the 17th century Reformed people started to play an increasingly important role in the life of a city mostly inhabited by Unitarians. Their growth had been advanced by the gifts of the *Calvinist* Transylvanian princes. They received the ruined church on Kolgălnicenau (then Farkas) Street, with the support of Gábor Bethlen, and with the help of György Rákóczi I they were able to rebuild it and furnish it with new pews and a pulpit. Prince Rákóczi brought expert stonemasons from the Baltic Sea who remade the vault. On July 1, 1647 a festive service was held in the reconstructed church building to consecrate it in the presence of the prince. A few years later a Reformed boarding school was built on land next to the church and became one of the best schools in Transylvania.

1660. János Linczigh, judge royal

The Turkish danger, previously known only by rumour, was experienced by the people of Cluj firsthand and to their cost in the year 1660.

When György Rákóczi II turned against the Turks, Seidi *Pasha* was sent to Transylvania to punish him. Reaching the walls of Cluj, the pasha wanted to occupy the city that promised much rich plunder.

The people of Cluj sent János Linczigh, the judge royal, as an ambassador to conciliate the Turk with gifts. However, the insatiable pasha threatened to kill the judge if he did not open the gates of the city before the *janissaries*. When the wise Linczigh reached the Mănăștur gate escorted by janissaries, in order that they would not understand, he shouted to the guards in *Latin* that they must keep the enemy out. When the Turks threatened him, he called out in Hungarian, "Now I must die, but don't surrender the city."

Unable to get the gates open, the Turks had to make do with the gifts and leave. Cluj was saved from destruction thanks to the judge royal, who risked his own life for his city.

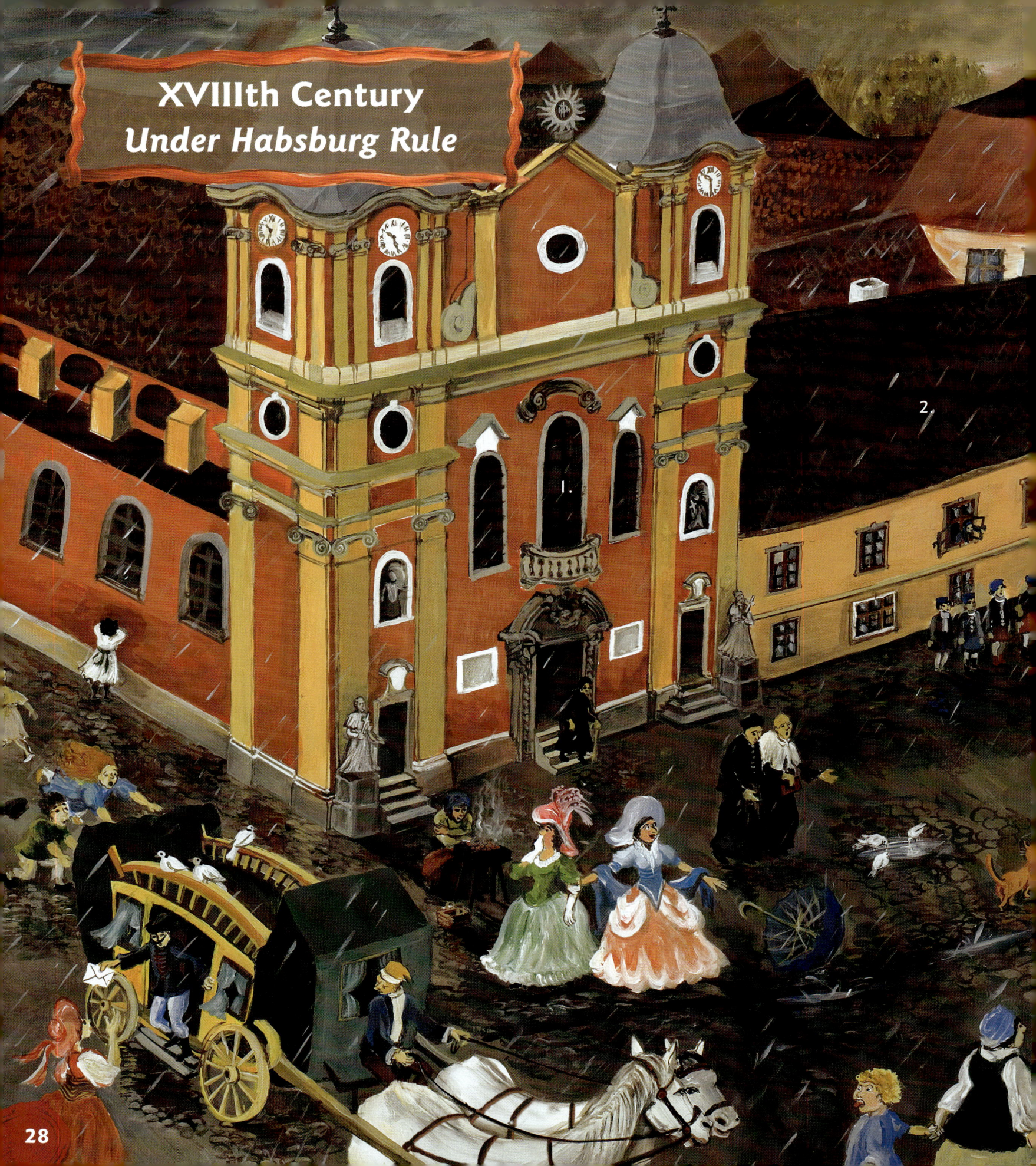

XVIIIth Century
Under Habsburg Rule

A new age in the life of Cluj began at the beginning of the 18th century when Transylvania came under *Habsburg* rule. The streets of Cluj were filled with Austrian soldiers and the first mail-coach entered the city. Later, the *main government office* was located there, and thus Cluj became the centre or rather the capital of Transylvania. Due to the support of the emperor, the Catholic religion, especially the Jesuit order, entered the daily life of the city again. New churches were built and the Catholics refurbished the interior of St. Michael's Church. Long lines of carts jogged along towards the centre of the city, carrying stones to the beginning of Kogălniceanu Street where the Jesuit church, friary and college were under construction. The Jesuits offered a boarding house near the college to the young noblemen who studied with them. However, the famous college attracted so many students that the boarding house soon came to be too small, and so the Báthory-Apor *Seminary* was built. After the plague epidemic came to an end in approximately 1739, a decorative, *Baroque* statue representing the Virgin Mary was built as a sign of gratitude in the middle of the square surrounded by the college, church, boarding house and seminary. This Jesuit centre, echoing with the noise of their students, became a point of pride for the city.

1. Jesuit (later the Piarist) Church; 2. friary and college; 3. noblemen's boarding house; 4. Mary Statute; 5. Báthory-Apor Seminary.

Between the Kuruc and the Labanc

News of the War of Independence led by Ferenc Rákóczi II against Habsburg rule soon spread throughout the country. *General* Rabutin, the Transylvanian commander of the Habsburg imperial troops, ordered such a huge garrison to Cluj that, according to historians, horses were stabled not only in the courtyards, but sometimes even inside the houses.

There was not much fruit in the hostats in the year 1704. At the beginning of the year the outskirts were burnt by the *Kuruc* besieging the city and in the fall the *Labanc* attacked. The roar of cannons was heard day and night and the walls of the fortress shook. The people were robbed of everything. Their houses were burnt down and in their courtyards, imperial soldiers roasted their pigs and cattle. One of the historians of the age wrote: "When the War of Independence ended in 1711, having suffered under both armies, Treasure-Cluj was transformed into Beggar-Cluj."

1735. The Citadel

In 1714 the imperial *war engineer* Giovanni Morando Visconti arrived to the city to make drawings and surveys for a *fortification*, the Citadel, which was to be built for the Austrian army. The fortification was planned for the other side of the river Someș, on the hill opposite the city of Cluj. On May 1715 Count Steinville, Transylvania's military commander, organized a grand celebration to mark the start of the work. However the political situation did not favour rapid construction, and when the Citadel was finally finished in 1735, after the death of Visconti, it was outdated as a defence. The new *artillery* of the age could have conquered the fortification easily. Having an irregular pentagon shape and strengthened on its corners with bastions, it was important mainly because it was built on a location from where the city could be easily kept under control.

1786. The Bánffy Palace

In the early spring of 1774, to the great surprise of the people, some of the houses behind St. Michael's Church were demolished. It soon became known that Count György Bánffy, Transylvania's governor, had asked Sibiu's chief architect, Johann Eberhart Blaumann, to design a palace which would be more magnificent than any other building in Cluj on the site of the demolished houses. According to the contract, he promised not less than 12,000 Rhenish gold coins, 200 bottles of wine and 50 *bushel*s of wheat to the architect for his work. In barely a year the front of the palace, which had a triple entrance and columned balcony, was built. However, the construction consumed terrible amounts of money and it was not until twelve years later that it was inaugurated. The Baroque palace with its spacious, inner courtyard was the most modern building of the city. Both friends and rivals admired and envied its white-gold rooms decorated with silk tapestry, enormous Venetian mirrors and family portraits.

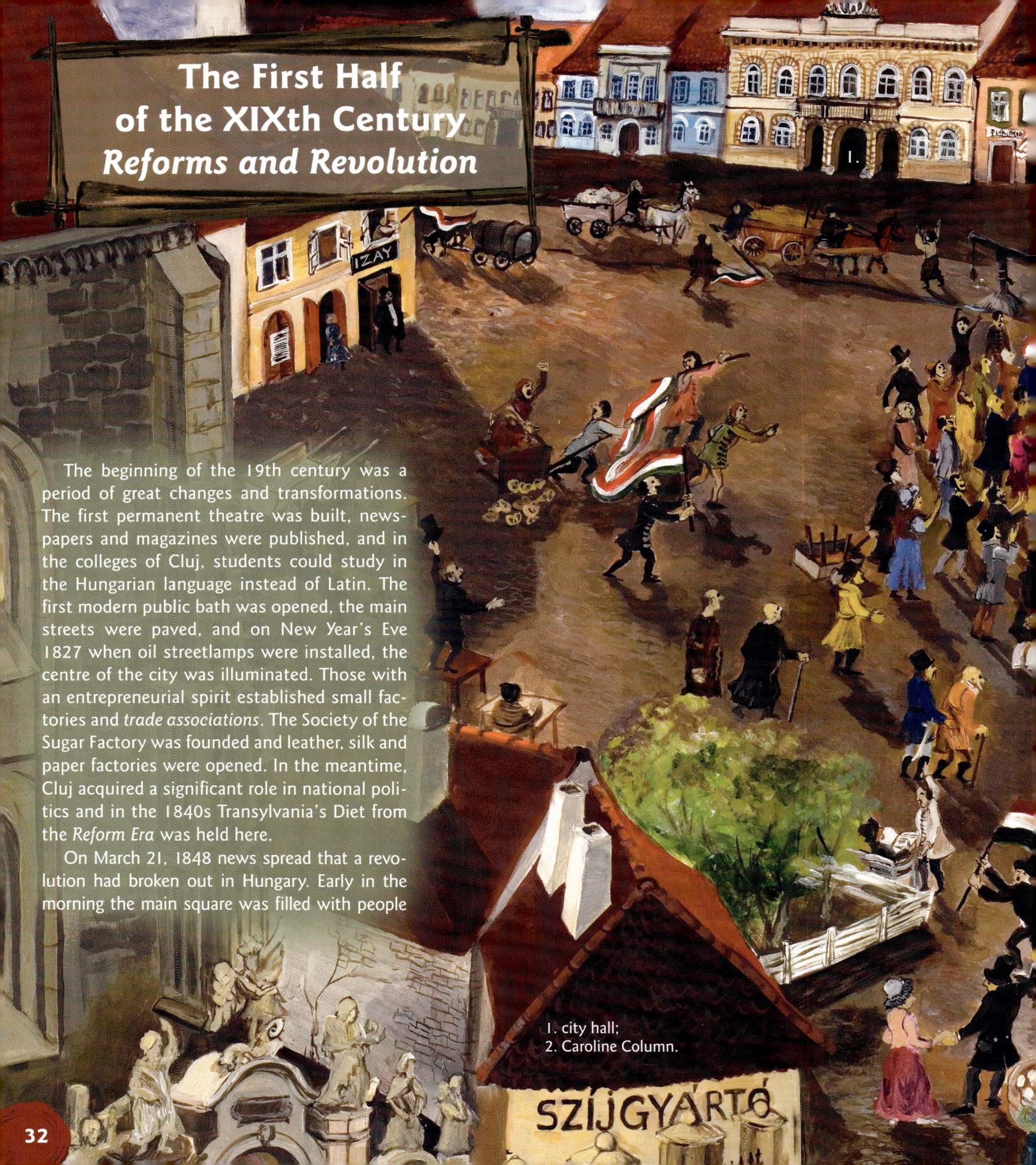

The First Half of the XIXth Century
Reforms and Revolution

The beginning of the 19th century was a period of great changes and transformations. The first permanent theatre was built, newspapers and magazines were published, and in the colleges of Cluj, students could study in the Hungarian language instead of Latin. The first modern public bath was opened, the main streets were paved, and on New Year's Eve 1827 when oil streetlamps were installed, the centre of the city was illuminated. Those with an entrepreneurial spirit established small factories and *trade associations*. The Society of the Sugar Factory was founded and leather, silk and paper factories were opened. In the meantime, Cluj acquired a significant role in national politics and in the 1840s Transylvania's Diet from the *Reform Era* was held here.

On March 21, 1848 news spread that a revolution had broken out in Hungary. Early in the morning the main square was filled with people

1. city hall;
2. Caroline Column.

and the more courageous students of the three colleges and the city's apprentices poured out excitedly into the streets. Protesters, led by young intellectuals, pinned rosettes to their chests and waving the national flag they sang the "Szózat" ("Appeal", a poem by Mihály Vörösmarty, regarded as the second Hungarian National Anthem), and recited Sándor Petőfi's "Nemzeti dal" ("National Song"). Posters listed the most important demands. Changes demanded by the great assembly were codified at the end of May by the Diet held in the *Redut* on Memorandumului Street: serfs were emancipated, the *freedom of the press* was proclaimed, it was decided that railways would be built, and a *union* was declared between Transylvania and Hungary. The *Greek-Catholic* religion was also recognized.

However Cluj could not escape the bloody events of the War of Independence and the oppression that followed it.

1800. The Greek-Catholic Church in the centre

From the 18th century, the Romanian population had played an increasingly important role in the life of the city. One sign of their influence can be seen in the fact that they were able to build new churches. In 1795 on the hill west of Hajongard cemetery, they finished the *Orthodox Church* built with the generous donations of Greek merchants living in the city. A few years later the *Greek-Catholics* built their own church close to the main square. In 1800 Bishop Ioan Bob from Blaj, who had supported the construction generously, also participated in the consecration ceremony of the church.

At a ball.

1817. The imperial visit

The most memorable event for the 18,000 inhabitants of the city took place in 1817. On August 18 Emperor Francis I and his wife, Caroline Augusta, visited the city. This was the first time a Habsburg monarch had come to Cluj. The people welcomed the imperial carriages and fancy entourage enthusiastically, and escorted the imperial couple to their residence at the Bánffy Palace. In the following days, while the emperor was occupied with the affairs of the city, the empress helped the downtrodden, donating to the poor and giving a significant amount of money to the city hospital.

The people of Cluj often spoke of the imperial visit and later they erected an obelisk called the Caroline Column in the main square to commemorate the event.

1834. Bánk bán in Farkas Street

The first permanent Hungarian Theatre Company, the Hungarian Noble Theatre Company of Transylvania, was established in 1792. At first it held its performances in the upper story of the Rhédey house which stood at the southwest corner of the main square. The first theatre building in Transylvania was finished in 1821 on Farkas (now Kolgălniceanu) Street. Famous actors from Transylvania and Hungary appeared on its stage. The Transylvanian premiere of József Katona's historical drama *Bánk bán* was held here in 1834 and became one of the most beloved plays of Hungarian theatres. The Cluj theatre soon became a favourite place of amusement for the educated audience of the city.

The Second Half of the XIXth Century
Peace and Prosperity

After the *Austro-Hungarian Compromise* the main government office was closed down, and Cluj lost its role as the capital of the Principality of Transylvania. However, it did not relapse into the status of a provincial town. By the 1880s its population had increased to 30,000, it had seven factories, the first steam engine roared into the city, and the old oil streetlamps were replaced with modern gas lamps. By the end of the century the shabby stalls around St. Michael's Church had been demolished, and from that time on, people could walk on paved *promenade*s. The favourite amusement place of the city was created in the old Rákóczi garden. Spacious walkways surrounded by trees intersected in what came to be known as Central Park. During the summer, swans glided upon the lake and young couples boated, while in the winter ice-skaters had their turn. In front of the splendid building of the Casino, there was a fountain and a little music pavilion, where military bands entertained the audience on a regular basis.

1. Casino; 2. music pavilion.

Coffee shops and promenades

The promenade was the most significant venue of 19th century city life. It was the place for gossip, but also for doing important business. On weekends, the promenades around St. Michael's Church bustled with activity, as did Ferenc Deák (now Eroilor) Street. Everybody showed up: pipe-smoking gentlemen, pretty ladies, blushing girls, and giggling maids. Gipsies who knew all the modern tunes of the time played popular music.

In the heat of the summer, if they became tired of walking, people could rest in the shade on the terrace of one of the many coffee shops. In the main square and in the surrounding area where the more elegant cafes of the city were located, coffee, milk and cakes were served. While drinking coffee, it was also possible to play cards or pool, and the most important newspapers could be browsed in nearby reading rooms. The most distinguished coffee shop was the New York Literary Café and Hotel (later, the Hotel Continental) which stood on one of the corners of the main square.

1872. Franz Joseph University

After the Compromise, Transylvania was united with Hungary, so the country increased in size and needed another university besides the one in Budapest. Cluj had been competing with Bratislava for some time for the honour of having Hungary's second university, and in the end the city on the banks of the Someș proved a better choice in many respects. It was not just that Cluj was already home to three famous schools. There was also the building vacated by the main government when it left, which was given to the new university. The founding of EME (the Transylvanian Museum Association) in 1859 also influenced the decision-making, because the organization's rich library, spacious *botanical garden*, and precious museum collections all supported a university education. The university, established in 1872, was named after the Austrian emperor and Hungarian king, Franz Joseph. On the opening day of the academic year, university professors and important city individuals were invited to a festive dinner in the main hall of the Redut, and in the evening a special performance was held in the theatre. In the final years of the century, the construction of a modern building for the university was begun and was not completed until the beginning of the 20th century.

The Jews of Cluj

In 1623 Gábor Bethlen issued a document that permitted Jews to settle down, to trade and to profess their religion freely throughout the whole territory of Transylvania. Although initially they were allowed to build houses only at the outskirts of Cluj, in time they were granted the opportunity to move into the centre as well. By the end of the 19th century, their number had increased to 4,000. Due to their famous inventiveness, the Jews became the city's most well-known entrepreneurs. The story of Vilmos Fischer, the president of the Jewish community of Cluj, is one of the most interesting. He won worldwide fame at the 1867 Paris World's Fair representing the Transylvanian porcelain industry with his multi-coloured, golden porcelain pieces. The Jews were different from the rest of the inhabitants of Cluj primarily in their religion. In their religious meeting houses, called synagogues, Jewish men with caps and *side lock*s read the *Torah*. Traditional Jewish weddings offered an interesting sight too. The young couple standing underneath a *chuppah* took an oath to remain eternally faithful to each other, while guests danced around them. During the ceremony the groom stamped on a glass with his feet, and guests took the pieces home as a remembrance of the wedding.

The Beginning of the XXth Century
Life at the Turn of the Century

In the summer of 1902, pieces of the Matthias statue that still stands in the main square today, were unloaded from boxcars arriving from Budapest. Where once there had been a small depot, a new railway station worthy of the significance of the city now stood. In front of the station building, on Gábor Baross Square (now, Piața Gării) *omnibus*es, *carriage and pair*s, and *hansom cab*s formed a line, and a small steam tram proclaimed with a loud whistle that it had started its journey towards the main square and the Beer Factory. The turn of the century witnessed a period of elegant civilian life, of industry and commerce, and also a lively cultural life. In 1910 the Urania Palace, a purposed-designed movie theatre seating 500, was built. In 1911 the Marianum, a Catholic girl's educational institution, was consecrated. Banks and insurance companies were opened, hotels were built, and the new building for the university and Hungary's most modern university library were also inaugurated. In the Mikó garden, a district with medical clinics was created, and hospitals with modern equipment were opened one after the other.

Although the outbreak of *World War* I did not bring the hustle and bustle of city affairs to a halt, the everyday life of Cluj was thoroughly changed by the political events of the period that followed.

1. train station;
2. steam tram.

1902. Matthias statue

The main square, which had been rid of street vendors less than two years earlier and paved with *basalt cobblestones*, was filled with gentlemen with walking-sticks and ladies with parasols. After the ceremonial speeches, the statue was unveiled. Members of the statue committee noted with satisfaction that their decision to choose the piece by the Bratislava-born János Fadrusz, from the seven works submitted for their consideration, had been perfectly justified. The citizens of Cluj had surmised this too since news had spread that a previous version of the statue had enjoyed a great success at the 1900 Paris World's Fair. According to tradition, the figure of King Matthias on horseback is surrounded by Generals Balázs Magyar and Pál Kinizsi on the left and *Voivode* István Báthory and *Palatine* István Szapolyai on the right. The huge bronze statue commemorated the great son of the city in a fitting manner, and since then has become the single most important symbol of Cluj.

1906. The new National Theatre

In June the old theatre in Farkas (now Kogălniceanu) Street closed its gates. Just two months later, hansom cabs waited to carry home evening theatre goers in Hunyadi Square (now, Piața Ștefan cel Mare). The new National Theatre building, which seated 1,300, was the work of the Viennese company "Fellner und Helmer", the most fashionable theatre and casino design firm of the monarchy. The building hosted the Hungarian theatre company until 1919. At one side of the theatre building stood the elegant Judicial Palace, and at the other side the Thália coffee shop opened for business and became a daily meeting place for theatre lovers, prima donnas, and musicians. Flower shops dotted the area and enthusiastic admirers with large bouquets could be seen heading towards the theatre's stage door even late in the evenings. The neighbourhood of the theatre also offered daytime attractions, to the great delight of young students living in the nearby Teachers' House.

Pathé film-making camera from 1913

1913. Film studio at Central Park

Jenő Janovics, director of the National Theatre of Cluj, saw a good business opportunity in film. He opened a movie theatre and in 1913 he established a film studio in the building of the Summer Theatre Company by Central Park. Later he built a bigger film studio in nearby Florești, which came to be known as Movie Village. He made a contract with the French Pathé company to obtain good equipment and excellent professionals. The most well-known film from his studio was 1913's *Sárga csikó* (Yellow Colt) which was presented in many countries, including Japan. There were more than seventy films made in Janovics' studio with famous actors from Cluj and Budapest shooting scenes in Cluj. Unfortunately we know only of four surviving films: *A vén bakancsos és fia, a huszár* (The Old Foot Soldier and His Son, the Hussar), *Világrém* (World Horror), *A tolonc* (The Evicted) and the incomplete *Az utolsó éjszaka* (The Final Night) directed by Janovics himself. Mihály Kertész, the director of *A tolonc*, started his career in Cluj, and later became world famous under the name Michael Curtiz with the film *Casablanca*. Silent movie production in Cluj was ended by the difficult economic and political situation following World War I.

From the 1920s to 1940s
Between Two World Wars

From 1914 onwards, peacetime was followed by three decades full of interesting events. The keys and offices of the city changed hands several times. World War I ended in 1918, the Austro-Hungarian Monarchy was dissolved, and the Romanian royal army marched into Cluj on Christmas Eve. Under Romanian leadership, both the National Theatre and the university lost their former directors, and teaching staff and students moved to Szeged, Hungary. However Hungarian high schools continued to operate and Cluj became the capital of Hungarian journalism in Transylvania. Everyday life speeded up. Carriages destroyed in the war were replaced by more and more taxi cabs and autobuses. Cluj was considered the capital of Transylvania both by Hungarians and Romanians.

Then, World War II broke out and in September 1940, under the leadership of Governor Miklós Horthy, the Hungarian army entered the city. The soldiers were received with cheering and *kürtőskalács* (funnel cake) by the Hungarian inhabitants, while a large number of Romanians fled the city. For four years, Cluj was part of Hungary, and during this time many important institutions were built and several streets were cobbled. Even today, one can find man-hole covers with the inscription *Kolozsvár kir. városi vízművek* (Cluj royal city waterworks).

In the spring and summer of 1944 Hungary, and so Cluj too, was occupied by the Germans. The brick-factory was designated a *ghetto* and the Jewish population forced to live there. Later they were deported to the Auschwitz *death camp*. On the night of June 2, English-American forces bombarded the railway station and the surrounding area. In October the German and Hungarian armies left the city, with the Soviet army arriving in their place shortly after. With the end of World War II, Cluj and all of Transylvania became part of Romania again.

Under Romanian leadership

Between the two world wars Cluj was led by Romanian mayors. The image of the city changed a lot in this period. In 1923 at Bocskai Square (now, Piața Avram Iancu), across from the present day Romanian National Theatre, the Orthodox *Cathedral* in *neo-Byzantine* style was built. On the south-west corner of the square the Albina Palace was also constructed. The ground level held the Astra movie theatre and the Perry Ford car showroom, while on the first floor there was a Romanian bank.

The number of Romanian students increased. In the building of the Franz Joseph University, the Romanian King Ferdinand I University was also established. So many Romanian students enrolled that the permanent theatre building on Farkas (now Kogălniceanu) Street was demolished, and an Academic College, with a conference room that seated 1,000, was built.

1930. Long-distance autobus station

In 1930 the city council decided to open the first long-distance autobus station on the square behind the main Post Office. The new long-distance routes covered regions where there were no trains, so villages and small towns that had been inaccessible before were now included in the transportation system of the country. Traffic became more and more intense at the bus station. This is where keepers of market stalls arrived with their merchandise from the surrounding villages, and where girls from outside the city came to find work as maids. Thanks to the new bus services, more and more people came to work in the Cluj leather, beer, and porcelain factories too.

1944. Saving the Jews

The name of the Catholic Áron Márton was familiar to the citizens of Cluj. He was an academic priest, then a parish priest of the city, and in 1939 he was ordained as bishop of Transylvania in St. Michael's Church. On May 18, 1944, after Jews had been confined to the ghetto, he was the first Hungarian church leader to sharply criticize this inhumane policy from the pulpit. He also addressed the chief police officer of Cluj and the leaders of the Hungarian government in a letter, calling on them to stop the *deportation* or resign. In those days, together with his fellow priests, some brave university teachers, professors of medicine, and ordinary people, he organized the hiding of several hundred Jews.

Lawyer Aurel Socol organized the passage of Jews fleeing through Romania, while Professor Imre Haynal hid them in his clinic. The latter hospitalized them under false names or hid them in *air-raid shelter*s and saved hundreds of Jews from the death camps. Sometimes under the guise of darkness or air-raids, Haynal sneaked in to his Jewish patients to examine them or give them medical care. His only fear was that the nurses would let something out accidentally that the *Gestapo* or the police might hear. He asked Áron Márton for assistance and the bishop gave a sermon in the clinic's chapel on the serious sin of careless talk.

The Second Half of the XXth Century
The Concrete City

1. the historic Calvaria Catholic Church in Mănăștur;
2. Mănăștur overpass.

1.

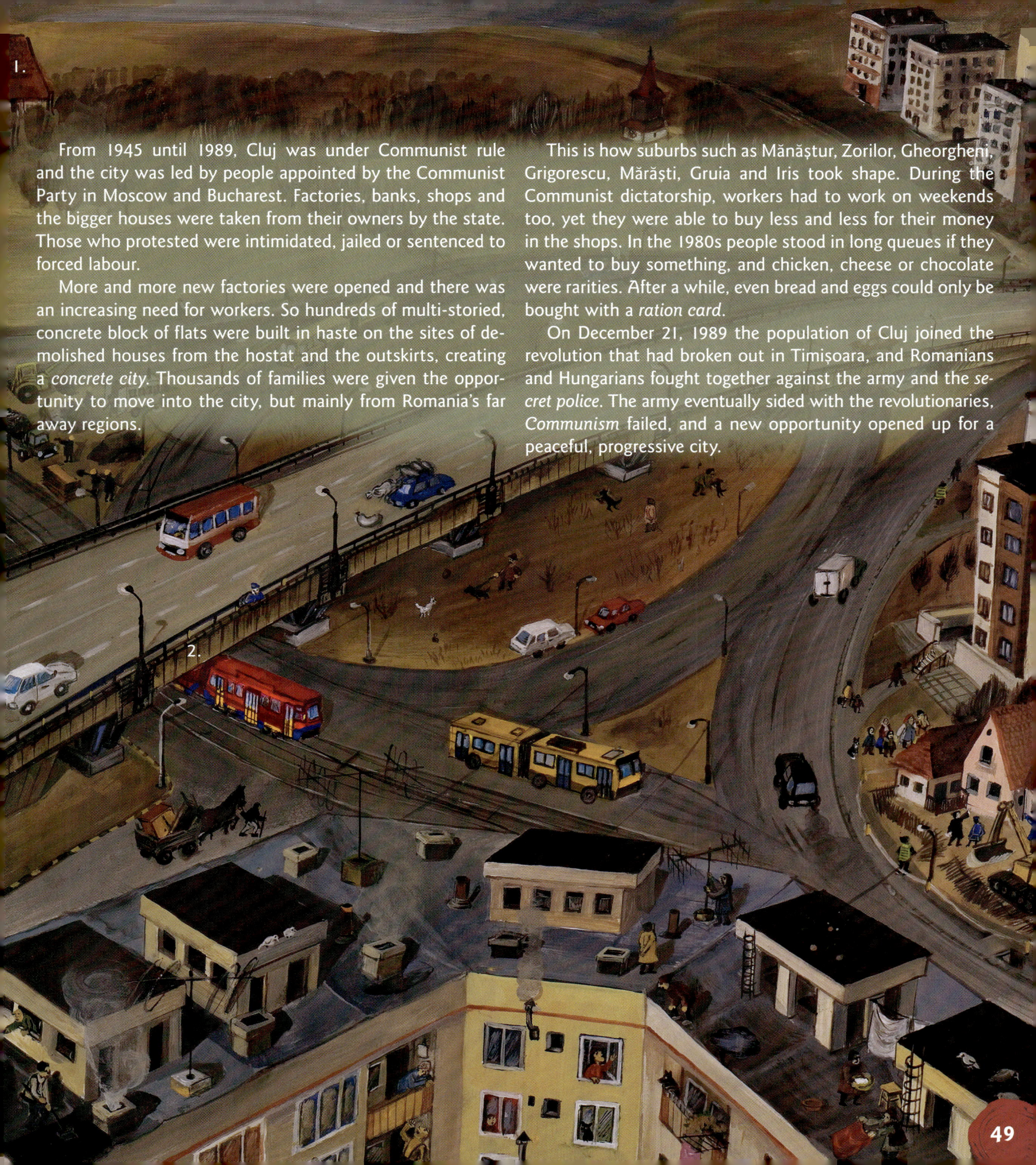

From 1945 until 1989, Cluj was under Communist rule and the city was led by people appointed by the Communist Party in Moscow and Bucharest. Factories, banks, shops and the bigger houses were taken from their owners by the state. Those who protested were intimidated, jailed or sentenced to forced labour.

More and more new factories were opened and there was an increasing need for workers. So hundreds of multi-storied, concrete block of flats were built in haste on the sites of demolished houses from the hostat and the outskirts, creating a *concrete city*. Thousands of families were given the opportunity to move into the city, but mainly from Romania's far away regions.

This is how suburbs such as Mănăştur, Zorilor, Gheorgheni, Grigorescu, Mărăşti, Gruia and Iris took shape. During the Communist dictatorship, workers had to work on weekends too, yet they were able to buy less and less for their money in the shops. In the 1980s people stood in long queues if they wanted to buy something, and chicken, cheese or chocolate were rarities. After a while, even bread and eggs could only be bought with a *ration card*.

On December 21, 1989 the population of Cluj joined the revolution that had broken out in Timişoara, and Romanians and Hungarians fought together against the army and the *secret police*. The army eventually sided with the revolutionaries, *Communism* failed, and a new opportunity opened up for a peaceful, progressive city.

2.

felvonuló pionírok

The mysterious house on Republicii Street

Republicii Street nr. 23 was the headquarters of the Romanian secret police. In the multi-storied basement of the building they interrogated any who had the courage to raise their voices against the Communist regime. While some were being questioned in the windowless cells, those who were next in line had to wait on their knees in the dark alley outside. Decades later the secret police building on Republicii Street became a *Pioneer House*, an institution for school children. The life of those children was rather different than that of children today. They could not get too attached to watching TV, because there was only one TV channel and only two hours' worth of programming every day. Of the two hours, only ten minutes was given for cartoons. Children were enrolled in different groups and spent their free time in the Pioneer House. They played with model airplanes, raced *go-kart*s, and learnt pottery, ballet, piano, or drawing. Many loved to go there and had no idea of the terrible things that had taken place in the house a few years earlier.

When the president of the country, Nicolae Ceaușescu, visited the city, children had to greet the "great party leader" with poems and songs learnt at the Pioneer House. Holding national flags and photographs of Ceaușescu, they had to march in front of him at the city stadium or at the *grandstand* built across from the National Theatre. These events usually took place during the summer vacation on the Communist holiday of *August 23*.

December 21, 1989

Cluj citizens heard about the revolution that had broken out in Timișoara from Kossuth Rádio and *Radio Free Europe*. At noon on December 21, 1989 workers and students gathered at a few points throughout the city and demanded the dismissal of the dictator Ceaușescu. At Piața Unirii (Libertății in Communist times), right in front of the Hotel Continental, the protesting crowd faced armed soldiers. Following orders, the army opened fire and many young people who were standing at the front lost their lives. Several others died at Hotel Astoria (where the Chamber of Commerce and Industry functions now) and the Beer Factory. On December 22, Ceaușescu fled the capital. However sporadic fighting and protests lasted throughout the whole country until Christmas. With the contribution of both Romanians and Hungarians the *National Salvation Front* was established in Cluj, as in most of the country's big cities.

The "Tricoloured" city

After 1990 mayors could be elected freely again. By 1992 Gheorghe Funar had been mayor of Cluj for twelve years. The installation of the newest statues and memorial plaques, and the covering of the whole city in the Romanian national colours, are linked with his name. From every lamppost there fluttered a Romanian flag that gathered dirt all year round. Every bench in the main square, in Central Park, and in playgrounds was painted red, yellow and blue. Even the jungle gyms and swings were covered with the colours of the national flag. The mayor's most astonishing order was to paint the garbage cans and roadside curbs in red, yellow and blue as well. This was too much, even for the Romanian population, since all the while the mayor was neglecting the maintenance and lighting of streets and the general improvement of the city. So in the 2004 elections the population of Cluj withdrew their support from Mayor Funar. His plan to make Piața Avram Iancu, which he had transformed and embellished, into the city's focal point had failed. Instead students and lovers still meet at the main square, Piața Unirii.

The Beginning of the XXIth Century and the Future
The European City

From 2004 onwards the city has taken on a new lease of life. In order to manage growing plane traffic a new *airport terminal* was built. Since 2011 fans have been able to watch their favorite football matches at the new Cluj Arena stadium that holds 30,000, and international stars have staged concerts in the new, multifunctional hall there. After a match or concert, they can get on the new, purple, low to the ground trams and travel towards Mănăștur or the railway station.

The streets in the centre were paved again and given new lighting. Nowadays, electric cables for the lights are often put underground instead of being strung from one lamppost to the next. In several parts of the city, new suburbs, office blocks, *industrial parks* and business centers emerged. Cluj, with its ten universities and almost a hundred thousand students, with its theatres, operas, philharmonics and more than twenty movie theatres, shines in its justifiable status as the capital of Transylvania. In 2015 it received the title of European Youth Capital, and in 2021 it hopes to obtain the European Capital of Culture title too.

Cluj, the festival city

Since 2002, every year at the beginning of June, TIFF (Transylvania International Film Festival) transforms Cluj into the European capital for film lovers. Filmtettfeszt (Hungarian Film Gathering of Transylvania), Comedy Cluj and other film festivals also enrich the offering. The city hosts the biennial Interferences International Theatre Festival and several classical and light music concerts as well. In the summer, the international music festival, Untold, attracts a vast number of visitors from around the country and abroad. Since 2012, St. Stephen's week and the Hungarian Days of Cluj draw not only current residents of Cluj and the neighbouring environs, but also former inhabitants of the city from all over the world.

The international airport in Someșeni

The first airplane landed on the *runway* at Someșeni in 1922. In 1933 the government in Bucharest internationalized the Cluj airport and on September 11 the Czech CSA airline's plane, a propellered Farman Goliath travelling from Prague to Bucharest with just ten people on board, landed in Cluj. By 2010 the Avram Iancu International Airport of Cluj had become the second busiest airport in the country. Every week a hundred flights take off from the runway to head to one of thirty destinations in Europe or the Middle East. The modern Airbus and Boeing airplanes that hold about 100-200 passengers, carry one and a half million travelers from the new facility.

1. Avram Iancu International Airport of Cluj; 2. Cluj Arena; 3. multifunctional hall; 4. new tram.

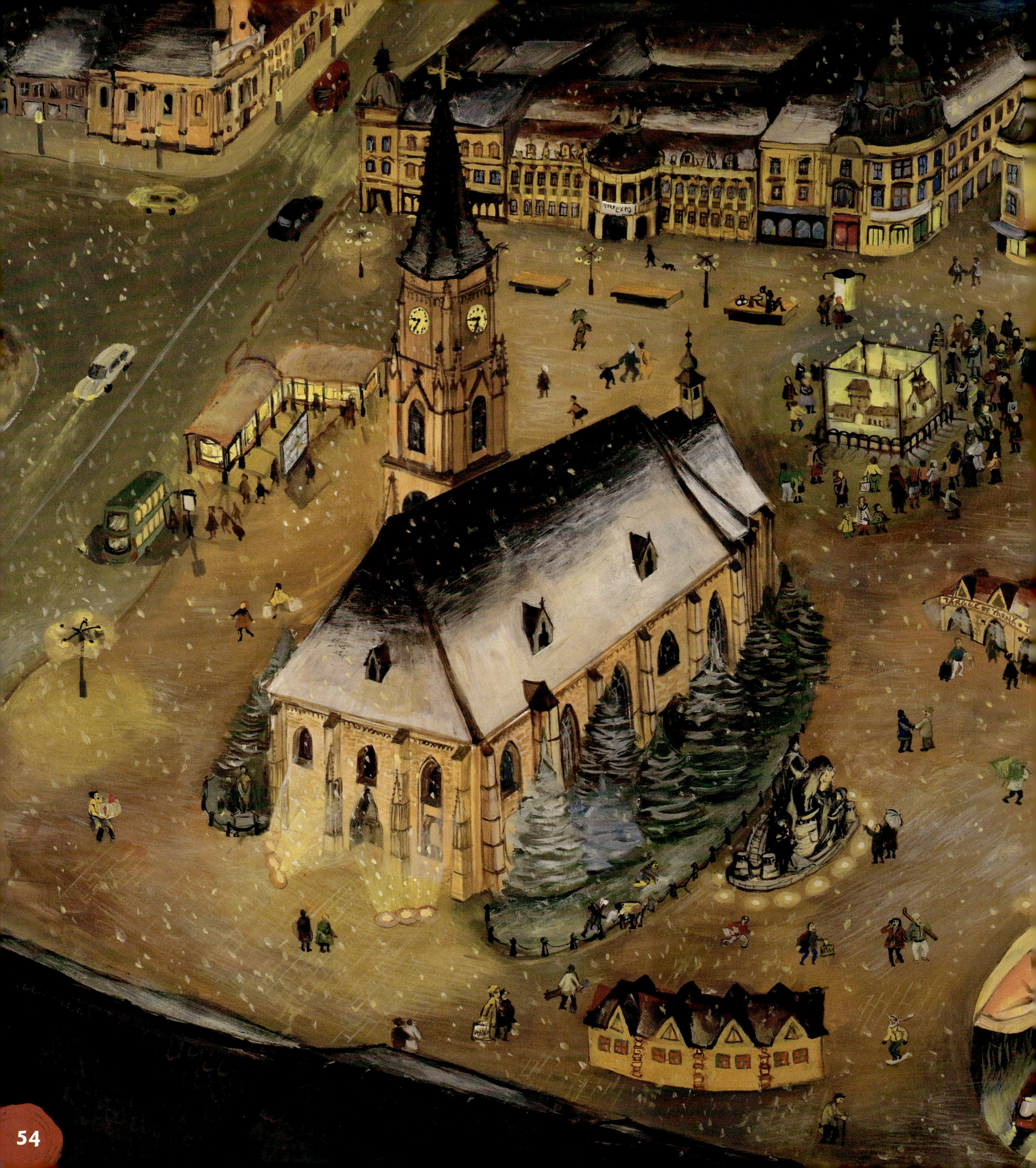

What will Cluj be like in ten, twenty, or fifty years' time? We can try to guess. We can imagine the city we would like to see and live in. Maybe you would also like to imagine it, because its development and growth may depend on you as you grow up.

Let's hope that in a few decades the blocks of flats built in Communist times will be empty. Most of them will be demolished, and bigger and more comfortable flats will be built in their places. According to existing plans, the city will soon annex the surrounding villages of Someșeni, Florești, Baciu and Gheorghieni, making them suburbs of the city. Maybe a fast metro line will be built underground that will cross the city in an east-west direction, and transport travellers from Florești to the International Airport in Someșeni.

Car traffic will be banned from most parts of the main square and Eroilor Street, so that the promenade of a hundred years ago will be revived. It will become again the place for walking, playing, and relaxing for all of Cluj's inhabitants and visitors.

1. restored Roman ruin;
2. metro station;
3. Eroilor Street.

55

Glossary

airport terminal – A building for receiving arriving and departing airline passengers. At the international terminals of the largest airports, there may be shops, restaurants and hotels in the terminal as well.

air-raid shelter – An underground or below-stairs structure offering protection against air-raids and bombings.

alms – Food or money given to beggars. In addition to donations from individuals, some monastic orders, such as the Dominican and the Franciscan orders, sustained themselves by asking for alms.

altar – A structure on which sacrifices are presented and celebrations are performed, and that creates an immediate connection between man and God.

amphitheatre – Two semicircular Roman theatres positioned facing each other and so forming a circle. The precursor of the modern circus, it was the arena where Roman gladiators performed and where fighters, or prisoners under death sentence, fought each other or wild animals. In the case of Napoca, we know of its existence, but we don't know its exact location.

amulet – According to superstition, a small object made of bone, stone, wood or some other material, often worn as a pendant around the neck, which has the power to protect its wearer from danger or evil.

artillery – A military unit that uses mounted projectile-firing guns or missile launchers.

Austro-Hungarian Compromise – After the suppression of the 1848 revolution, Hungary and Austria made an agreement, or compromise, and established a new state form, the Austro-Hungarian Monarchy.

August 23 – During World War II, Romania initially fought against the Axis armies (primarily Germany, Italy and Japan). Then, on August 23, 1944, a democratic opposition established a new government in Romania committed to the Allied armies (England, France, the United States, the Soviet Union and China) who opposed the Axis. When they came to power, the Romanian Communist party claimed credit for this switch to the Allied cause and under Communism, August 23 in Romania was a huge day of national celebration.

Avars – A nomadic people of Asian origin. The power of their empire, which included the Carpathian basin, stretched to the eastern parts of Europe too. As a result of the Avars' crusades, the Byzantine Empire paid them a very high tax for a considerable period of time. Attacks by the Bulgars and Franks, as well as internal conflicts, led to the decline of their empire around 900 A.D.

bailiff – An officer appointed by the king who was responsible for executing the decisions of the royal court.

Baroque – A period of artistic style that developed between 1600 and 1750. In Europe it was spread mainly by the Jesuits. Baroque buildings in Cluj include the Bánffy Palace, the Jesuit (later Piarist) Church, and the Minorite (Greek-Catholic) Church. The interior of St. Michael's Church in the main square is also in this style. Based on the characteristics of the art style, the word has been used also as an attribute to mean complicated, over-decorated, and exuberant.

basalt cobblestones – Dark grey, especially hard, round stones that were often used during the 19th century and at the beginning of the 20th for paving streets.

basilica – An oblong, roofed hall in ancient Roman towns or cities, which was originally a place for commercial activity, and later for courts of law.

Benedictine order – The first monastic order of the Roman Catholic Church. It was founded by Saint Benedict of Nursia in 529.

boarding school – A school where students live (i.e., eat and sleep), as well as having regular lessons.

botanical garden – A garden created for the cultivation, collection and display of rare plants.

bronze – A metal made by combining copper and tin, producing a material harder than copper.

bushel – a unit of weight used to measure agricultural goods such as wheat or potatoes.

Calvinists – Followers of John Calvin, the reformer from Geneva. In Transylvania, such people are usually called Reformed.

Capitolium – The Latin name of one of the hills of Rome. At the end of the 6th century B.C., a temple, also called the Capitolium, was built there in honour of the "Capitoline Triad": Jupiter, Juno and Minerva. Later, during the age of the Republic, temples based on the model of the Capitolium and called by the same name were built in the most prominent part of Roman cities and towns, usually in the forum.

carriage and pair – An elegant carriage pulled by two horses that awaited passengers at designated areas, like a modern day taxi. City transportation in Transylvania was by carriage and pair from the 18th to the beginning of the 20th century.

cathedral – The central, usually large, church in a diocese, an area ruled by a bishop.

charter – An official, sealed document in the Middle Ages.

chief judge, judge royal – In the 16th-17th centuries, the important cities of Transylvania were ruled by these two men who were city dwellers and who were elected by the city council. Since Cluj was populated mainly by Hungarians and Saxons, these two offices were held on an alternating basis by an individual from each group.

chuppah – A canopy under which a Jewish wedding ceremony is performed.

Cluj – The city has had several official names throughout the centuries. The Hungarian name for it is Kolozsvár, and the German is Klausenburg.

Communism – A political, social and economic system led by one single party, the Communist Party. Under this regime in Romania, individual rights of freedom, e.g., freedom of speech, were suppressed by the government, the practice of religion was forbidden, private property was dissolved, and industry, commerce and agriculture were all under full state control.

concrete city – A nickname for the grey suburbs built during the Communist regime out of prefabricated concrete elements.

cooper – A craftsman who makes containers out of narrow strips of wood that are bound together by two or more circles of metal, items such as wooden barrels, buckets, wash-basins, etc.

Dacians – A people group that lived in Dacia, approximately in what is the current region of Transylvania. Their appearance dates from around the 2nd century B.C. The gold and silver mines of the Carpathians represented their economic power. The separate Dacian tribes were united by Burebista around 60 B.C. During his reign, the Dacians conquered people living south and west of them, and represented a constant threat to the northern territories of the Roman Empire. After Burebista's death, due to internal fights, Dacian power weakened. Dacians tribes were united again by Decebal, and in 85 and 86 A.D. they defeated the Romans. Dacia was finally occupied by Traianus after two hard-fought conquests (101-102, 105) and a new Roman province, the Dacian Province, was founded on the occupied territories.

death camp – A detention camp created by the German Nationalist Socialists during World War II where the Jewish and Gipsy population was deported and killed. 5-6 million Jews and half a million of other nationalities died in the death camps.

deportation – The transportation and resettling of persons, families or groups considered dangerous from the perspective of the state to concentration camps, forced domicile or foreign lands.

devotional picture – A painting with a religious theme considered to have miraculous power.

Dominican order – A monastic order of the Roman Catholic Church founded by Saint Dominic in 1215.

evangelizing – The endeavour to convert pagans and people of other religions to one's own religious beliefs. Within Catholicism, this was usually the duty of monastic orders.

Fifteen Years War – The war against the Turks at the turn of the 17th century, when the opposing armies fought several bloody battles in Transylvania.

fortification - A fortress surrounded by walls designed for military and defense purposes developed after the appearance of fire guns. After 1711 following the strengthening of Habsburg power, fortifications were built throughout Transylvania in Cluj, Alba Iulia, Arad, and Timisoara.

Franciscan order – A preaching and alms-seeking monastic order, originating in the Roman Catholic Church, founded by Saint Francis of Assisi in 1209.

freedom of the press – Prior to the 1848 Revolution, a separate committee led by a so-called censor decided which books and newspapers could be published. One of the main goals of the Revolution was to abolish this and to obtain freedom to publish any kind of news or information.

friar – See **monk**.

garrison – A military unit commanded to protect a fortress or a fortified city.

general – A military officer of high rank.

Gepids – A people of Germanic origin, like their closest relatives, the Goths. Perhaps Jordanes, himself of Gothic origin, writes of them the most. He is considered the historian of ancient rival Gothic tribes and consequently his descriptions of the Gepids, most of which are disparaging, are suspect. Their territory from the 5-6th centuries, consisting of the Little Hungarian Plain and Transylvania with its centre in the Someș valley, was one of the most significant kingdoms of the time. Their dominion was ended by the Avars in 567.

Gestapo – the German Secret State Police from 1933 to 1945. The word is an abbreviation of the German expression *Geheime Staatspolizei*.

ghetto – A suburb or area of a city designated as a compulsory dwelling place for the Jewish population in World War II.

go-kart – A small, low to the ground, four wheeled vehicle powered by a gasoline engine and used for amusement and racing.

Gothic – The most significant art style of the Middle Ages, formerly called Lancet Gothic. The style is most represented by enormous cathedrals and by city parish churches and their decorations (wall paintings, altars, ornamented goldsmith's work, etc.). In Cluj, St. Michael's Church, the Central Reformed Church on Kolgăniceanu Street, and the Dominican Cloister (today a school building) were all built in the Gothic style.

Goth – The Goths were a Germanic people who conquered the Transylvanian territories in the middle of the 3rd century. After this, Gothic tribes separated into two branches. The Visigoths (Western Goths) settled in areas from Transylvania to the Dniester River, while the Ostrogoths (Eastern Goths) conquered regions east of the river until the Crimean Peninsula. In 376, right after defeating the Ostrogoths, the Huns beat Athanarik's Visigoth troops too. Later the two branches of the Goths confronted each other. The Ostrogoths fought on the side of the Huns, while the Visigoths were confederates of the Romans. Following the collapse of the Hun empire, both Gothic groups played a significant role in the shaping of European history.

grandstand – In Communist Romania, this was a stand reserved for party leaders from where they addressed the assembled population (workers, students, soldiers) on major state holidays.

Greek-Catholic Church – At the turn of the 18th century the Habsburg Empire, for political and religious reasons, supported the conversion of Romanians in Transylvania from the Eastern Orthodox Church to the Roman Catholic Church, and their acceptance of the pope's authority in Rome. Those who converted were called Greek-Catholics and received opportunities to study at Europe's most prestigious Catholic universities. The Greek-Catholic Church had a significant role in the formation of the Romanian intellectuals of Transylvania.

Habsburg – One of the most influential royal houses of Europe. The first king of Hungary of the Habsburg house occupied the throne in 1437. From the Battle of Mohács until the end of World War I, Hungary's king was a descendant of this house.

hansom cab – A two-wheeled carriage that accommodated two passengers. It was pulled by a single horse and the driver rode on top at the rear. Together with carriage and pairs, they fulfilled the role of taxis for the public.

hostat – The name for the suburbs derived from the German word, *Hochstadt*. Outside the walled city of medieval Cluj were several suburbs where, besides houses, there were stalls and gardens belonging to the city dwellers. Later, the north-eastern suburb of Cluj, where most houses had gardens, came to be called the Hostat. The inhabitants of this suburb made a living out of producing and selling vegetables and fruit.

Huns – A people of Asian origin. Their enormous military power can be seen in the building of the Great Wall of China which was considered necessary to repel them. At the beginning of the 5th century they conquered the Carpathian basin and created their centre of power somewhere in the southern part of the Great Hungarian Plain, in the area of the current city of Szeged. This is where Bleda (Buda) and Attila, the most important Hun ruler, lived. Their ravaging conquests against the divided Roman Empire were ended by Attila's death in 453. After this a power struggle broke out among Attila's sons, and Ellák (or according to Hungarian legends, Prince Csaba) won, but his weakened troops could not resist the attacks of former subjects. Germanic peoples forming an alliance, primarily the Gepids, defeated the Huns, and forced them to retreat. Later the Huns were integrated into the peoples of the eastern European steppe.

indulgence – A means of obtaining forgiveness of sin or a lessening of the punishment for sin in the Catholic church. To receive an indulgence, a person had to do something, perhaps pray a certain prayer or visit a certain place or perform a certain act.

industrial park – An area designated by the city where favourable conditions are offered to factories and companies (water and electricity is installed, waste removal is provided) to attract investors and create employment opportunities in the city.

janissaries – Soldiers in the standing army of the Turks. They were originally Christian children who had been kidnapped, converted to Islam, and trained to fight.

Jesuits – A Roman Catholic monastic order founded by Ignatius of Loyola in 1540. Their official name is the Society of Jesus. They are credited with the reorganization and strengthening of the Roman Catholic Church after the Reformation.

judge royal – See **chief judge, judge royal**

Kuruc – An anti-Habsburg Hungarian soldier fighting against the Habsburg occupation of Hungary. They fought against the Austrian army on the side of the "Kuruc king", Imre Thököly, and later from 1703 to 1711 in the anti-Habsburg War of Independence led by Ferenc Rákóczi II. Many "Kuruc songs" were written about their famous leaders Tamás Esze, Bottyán Vak and Ádám Balogh.

Labanc – The opponents of the Kuruc. They were paid soldiers of the army of the king of the house of Habsburg.

Latin – The language of ancient Romans which was used in Europe for centuries. Latin was the language of science, of university education, and of the Roman Catholic Church.

Liturgy of the Hours – The praying of the Liturgy of the Hours is the common prayer practice of Catholic monks, said seven times a day at specific times or hours.

Lutheran – A Christian denomination that traces its interpretation of the Christian religion to the teachings of Martin Luther.

main government office – The administrative authority of the Transylvanian Principality under Habsburg rule from 1691 to 1867.

monastery – A building where monks live and work together.

Mongols – A people originating in Central-Asia. Their empire was founded by Genghis Khan who united the (semi) nomadic tribes of the region. At the beginning of the 13th century they conquered northern China and Iran with their fast cavalry, defeated the Russian army at Kiev, and invaded India. After occupying Kiev, the Mongol troops lead by Batu Khan invaded Hungary. The battle of Mohi (today Muhi) on April 11, 1241 ended with the crushing defeat of King Bela IVth's troops. After ransacking most of the country, the Mongols withdrew at the end of 1241 and the rebuilding of Hungary could begin.

monk – A member of a church community living in a monastery. The everyday life of monks is determined by a certain rule and they usually make vows of poverty and obedience.

Napoca – A former Roman city at the site of modern Cluj, which the Romans may have taken over from the original inhabitants. It may be of Dacian or even Celtic origin, since no traces of a Dacian settlement have been found there to date. It's also possible that the name refers not to a particular settlement, but to the whole region. The first, small settlement ran from the present-day Morilor Canal to the Historical Museum.

National Salvation Front – The political organization which replaced the Romanian Communist government in the December 1989 revolution.

Neo-Byzantine – A style characteristic primarily of the architecture of the Eastern Orthodox Church and following the stylistic marks of Byzantine architecture.

omnibus – A public vehicle pulled by a horse and designed to carry several passengers, the predecessor of the autobus. The name is derived from the Latin *omnibus*, meaning, for everyone.

Orthodox (Eastern Orthodox) Church – The oldest Christian denomination next to the Roman Catholic Church. As the name suggests, it was established in the eastern part of the Roman Empire, in territories where Greek was the predominant language. After the "great schism" in 1054, it spread primarily in Eastern Europe.

palatine – A high ranking official attached to a royal or imperial court.

paper mill – A building where paper is made using hydropower (water power).

parish church – In the Middle Ages, the main church of a city or part of a city, whose priest could perform all the sacraments (baptism, confession, marriage, burial, etc.).

pasha – A title and rank in the Turkish Empire. Initially the title was given only to the sultan's sons, but later other significant leaders were allowed to use it also.

pastor – A Protestant preacher or minister is often called a pastor.

piața – a Romanian word meaning square or market place

pilgrim – A religious devotee who travels to a holy location (perhaps a church or a statue) and who is strengthened in his faith by doing so.

Pioneer House – The headquarters for the events and activities of the pioneers who were member of a youth organization that aimed to train children in a Communist and nationalistic spirit.

portcullis – A vertically moving grating of iron to defend doors and gates, frequently used in fortresses and fortifications.

praetorium – The headquarters of the Roman military general in the provinces; the residence of the Roman governor.

principality – A state ruled over by an elected monarch who bears the title of prince. The formation of the independent Transylvanian Principality following the Battle of Mohács in 1526 lasted for decades. It was established in 1570 when the Hungarian kings of the Habsburg dynasty, reigning in the western and eastern parts of the Hungarian Kingdom of the Middle Ages, recognized the independence of the new state form created from the eastern provinces of the former kingdom. The central part of the former Hungarian Kingdom was occupied by the Turks.

privilege – Certain favors and obligations given to certain cities or peoples by the king.

proconsul – The person who represented imperial power in the provinces of the Roman empire.

promenade – A public space created for pedestrian traffic.

Protestant – The word derives from the Latin *protestatio*. In 1529, at the Imperial Diet of Speyer, Martin Luther's followers protested the imperial politics of religion. The title of the document summing up their grievances was *Protestatio*. From then on, the followers of the reformers were called Protestants.

pulpit – The place from which a preacher speaks in a Christian church. The raised stand against the northern wall of the church may be made of stone, marble or wood, and is often decoratively carved. A painted or sculptured canopy above provides a useful acoustic effect in projecting the preacher's voice to the congregation.

Radio Free Europe – A US funded broadcasting agency that transmits to countries where the free flow of information may be limited due to government censorship. Hungarian broadcasts were ended in 1993. Broadcasts in the Romanian language ended in 2008.

ration card - Certain hard to acquire foods were allocated in an equal way during Communist times. A ration card indicated how much of an item a person could buy, e.g., ½ kg bread and 1 l of milk per day, and 1 kg of flour, sugar, and oil per month.

Redut – An old French word meaning ball room. Diets in the Reform Era were organized in the large ball room of the house on Memorandului Street in Cluj that became known as the Redut.

refectory – The dining area of a monastery where the monks eat their common meals.

Reform Era - This is the period in Hungarian history before the Revolution of 1848. The name came from the endeavour to reform a country that was relatively behind the rest of Europe by implementing a series of new laws and establishing new institutions.

Reformation – On October 31, 1517 Martin Luther, a monk in the Augustinian order of the Roman Catholic Church, protested against the selling of indulgences in his Ninety-five Theses and demanded the renewal of the church based on the teachings of the Bible. His doctrines spread quickly. Soon after Germany, Switzerland, The Netherlands, France, and from 1540 Hungary and Transylvania also joined the Reformation.

Reformed Church – A Christian church founded on the teachings of Swiss and southern German Reformed preachers. In Transylvania the Reformed Church is the largest among the Protestant denominations.

renaissance – Literally, "rebirth", the revival of ancient art and culture. The new art style grew out of Italy in the 14th century, where many Renaissance buildings were erected, including palaces, churches, and town-halls. Later, Michaelangelo's world-famous paintings were made in this style too. The new style arrived in Cluj only in the 16th century, when the single-story Gothic houses of the city centre were replaced by two-storied, comfortable, beautifully decorated Renaissance houses.

Roman Catholic Church – One of the oldest Christian denominations and the largest, with members above one milliard. Catholic means universal. Their chief leader is the pope and according to tradition, the first bishop of Rome was the apostle Peter..

runway – The most important part of an airport, a 1-3 km long strip of ground covered by concrete, asphalt or a mixture of both, where planes take off and land.

sanctuary – The most important space of a church where the main altar is located and where the priests or ministers perform the church service.

seminary – A school, especially a theological school for the training of clergy.

secret police – Intelligence services or police operating in secret and as civilians who spied on the general population.

serf – A peasant obliged to work on the property of a wealthier landowner in the late Middle Ages and early modern times and who was not allowed to own land of his own.

side lock – A lock of hair worn in front of each ear in a hairstyle characteristic of male Jews who observe their traditions strictly.

Slavs – Ethnic groups of people who speak languages belonging to the Indo-European language family. Their land of origin is in the woodlands of northern Europe. From the 5th century their tribes gradually expanded west and south. As subjects of the Avars, they participated in the war against the Byzantine Empire and entered the Balkans as well. Later the Slavs were separated into three great branches that still exist today. The western branch includes the Polish, the Czechs and the Slovaks, the Eastern branch includes the Russians, the Ukrainians, the Belarusians and the Transcarpathian Ukrainians, and the Southern branch includes the Croatians, the Slovenians, the Serbs, the Bulgarians and the Macedonians.

spindle whorl – A small disc with a hole in the centre, usually made of clay. It fitted onto a spindle, which was used for spinning wool, increasing and maintaining its speed.

Torah – The texts of the five books of Moses which make up the first five books of the Christian Bible.

trade association – The successor of trade guilds, these were associations of craftsmen formed in the 19th century to further their collective interests.

trade guild – An association established to protect the interests of persons of the same trade.

Transylvanian Diet – A meeting consisting of chosen representatives who made decisions about the laws of Transylvania. During the time of the independent Transylvanian Principality, the Diet consisted of the representatives of three nations: the Hungarians, the Székelys and the Saxons.

union – The unification of two, formerly separate countries.

Unitarian – The Unitarian Church is the third largest group among the Protestant denominations of Transylvania. It was founded in Cluj by Pastor Ferenc Dávid. Unitarians deny the deity of Christ and the Holy Spirit, so they are often called anti-Trinitarian.

villa rustica – A villa in the countryside and the farm-buildings connected to it during Roman times. The wealthy inhabitants of Napoca moved to their villa rustica for weeks at a time several times a year, taking with them their family members, friends and slaves. Because of the warmer climate of that time, Napoca was considered an important wine producing region, so the grape harvest was the most important period of the year that households would spend at their villa rustica.

voivode – A local ruler or governor.

war engineer – A construction engineer who worked for the imperial army and designed military buildings.

wax impression – An imprint produced by a seal, usually made of metal, as it is pressed into melted wax.

world war – A war which involves many countries and covers a large part of the world. World War I occurred from 1914-1918, while World War II lasted from 1939-1945.

yurt – A dome-shaped building consisting of a wooden frame with a felt cover. This was the popular dwelling place for the conquering Hungarians. The yurt could be easily dismantled and transported and so was practical for nomadic communities.

Illustrations:
Andrea Jánosi

Vision and editing:
Balázs Zágoni

Historian and art historian editors:
Zsolt Kovács
Radu Lupescu
Melinda Mihály
Emese Sarkadi Nagy

Contributing authors:
Alexandru Diaconescu, Balázs Gergely, Attila Hunyadi, Zsolt Kovács, Radu Lupescu, Melinda Mihály, Emese Sarkadi Nagy, Balázs Zágoni

Publisher's reader: **András Kovács**
English language translators and editors: **Erzsébet Daray, Ailisha O'Sullivan**
Reproductions: **Diartis**
Image processing: **Carolina Banc**
Lay-out editor: **Ferenc Sütő**

Supporters:
Margit Barta, Ákos Egyed, Gábor Kerekes, Vilmos Kolumbán, Károly Lőwi, Márton Sarkadi, Orsolya Tóth, Emese Zsigmond, Entz Géza Foundation, Filmtett Association

Publisher:
Bálint Zágoni

© Andrea Jánosi, 2016
© Projectograph Ltd, 2016

Also in this series:

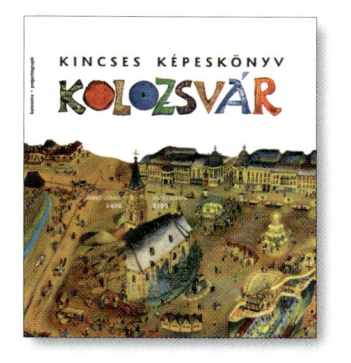

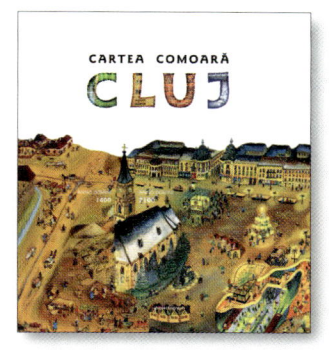

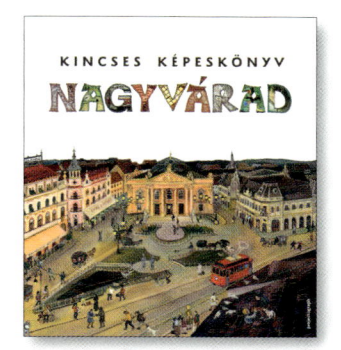

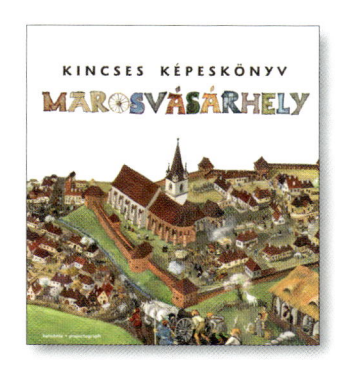

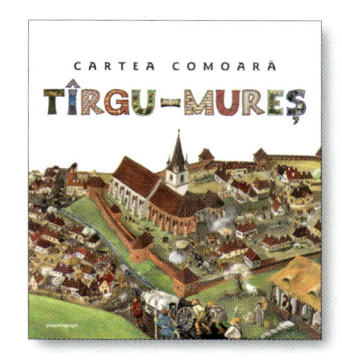

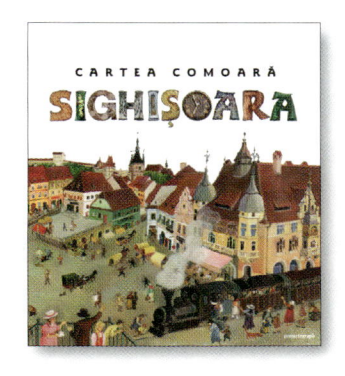

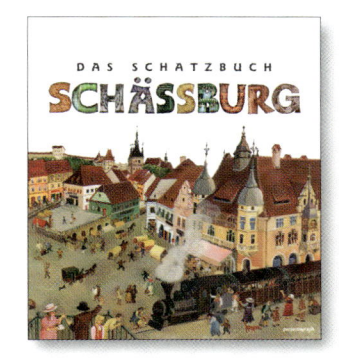

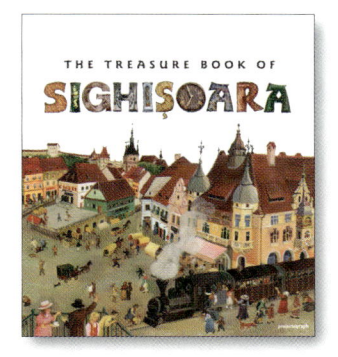

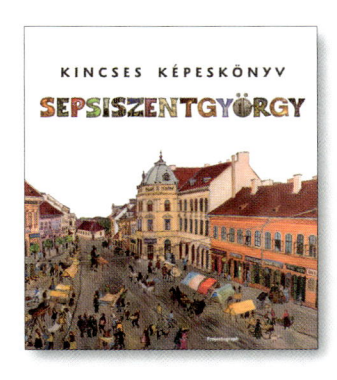

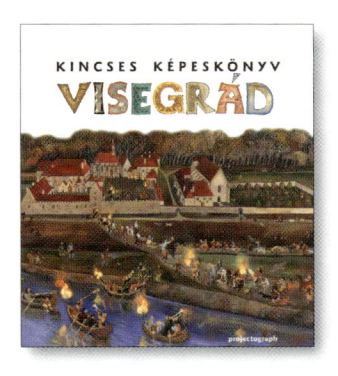

- KINCSES KÉPESKÖNYV — **KOLOZSVÁR**
- CARTEA COMOARĂ — **CLUJ**
- KINCSES KÉPESKÖNYV — **NAGYVÁRAD**
- KINCSES KÉPESKÖNYV — **MAROSVÁSÁRHELY**
- CARTEA COMOARĂ — **TÎRGU-MUREŞ**
- KINCSES KÉPESKÖNYV — **SEGESVÁR**
- CARTEA COMOARĂ — **SIGHIŞOARA**
- DAS SCHATZBUCH — **SCHÄSSBURG**
- THE TREASURE BOOK OF **SIGHIŞOARA**
- KINCSES KÉPESKÖNYV — **SEPSISZENTGYÖRGY**
- KINCSES KÉPESKÖNYV — **VISEGRÁD**
- KINCSES KÉPESKÖNYV — **SZÉKESFEHÉRVÁR**

Projectograph Ltd.

Tel: +40 720 547696, +40 745 583 669
projectograph@gmail.com
www.kincseskonyv.ro

Printed and bound at Dürer Printing House Ltd, Gyula, Hungary.

Descrierea CIP a Bibliotecii Naționale a României
ZÁGONI, BALÁZS
   The Treasure book of Cluj / Zágoni Balázs ; il.: Jánosi Andrea. -
Cluj-Napoca : Projectograph, 2016
   ISBN 978-606-94030-2-0

I. Jánosi, Andrea (il.)

94(498 Cluj-Napoca)